200 BLOCKS
from Quiltmaker
MAGAZINE

200 BLOCKS *from* Quiltmaker MAGAZINE

Original Patterns from Today's Top Designers

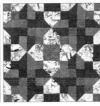

Martingale®
Create with Confidence

200 Blocks from *Quiltmaker* Magazine:
Original Patterns from Today's Top Designers
© 2012 from the Editors of *Quiltmaker* Magazine

Martingale®
19021 120th Ave. NE, Ste. 102
Bothell, WA 98011-9511 USA
ShopMartingale.com

Quiltmaker, ISSN 1047-1634, is published bimonthly by Creative Crafts Group, LLC, 741 Corporate Circle, Suite A, Golden, CO 80401, www.quiltmaker.com.

Printed in China
17 16 15 14 13 12   8 7 6 5 4 3 2 1

Library of Congress Cataloging-in-Publication Data is available upon request.

ISBN: 978-1-60468-167-3

MISSION STATEMENT
Dedicated to providing quality products and service to inspire creativity.

CREDITS
President & CEO: Tom Wierzbicki
Editor in Chief: Mary V. Green
Design Director: Paula Schlosser
Managing Editor: Karen Costello Soltys
Copy Editor: Sheila Chapman Ryan
Production Manager: Regina Girard
Cover and Text Designer: Paula Schlosser
Illustrator: Laurel Strand
Photographer: Mellisa Mahoney
Design Assistant: Connor Chin

Contents

200 Blocks— So Many Quilts!

The collection of blocks in this book will add so much to your quiltmaking toolbox. Each block was made by one of today's top quilt designers—and they are a talented group of quilters. The blocks come in a variety of techniques and styles—all for your quilting pleasure! Simple blocks, challenging blocks, and works of arts. Contemporary, traditional, and whimsical. You'll find inspiration and ideas for every quilt you want to make.

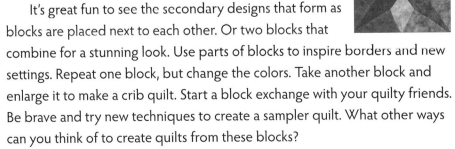

All of the appliqué patterns, embroidery designs, and patterns needed for piecing, foundation piecing, or English paper piecing are included

full-size on the enclosed CD. Use the handy block tab to select and then print the patterns as you need them.

All of the blocks—pieced, appliquéd, or mixed media—will finish at 12", so keep in mind this means each block will be 12½" until you sew it into your project. To help you plan an entire quilt made of 12" blocks, we've included general yardage information for various size quilts and settings, starting on page 115.

It's great fun to see the secondary designs that form as blocks are placed next to each other. Or two blocks that combine for a stunning look. Use parts of blocks to inspire borders and new settings. Repeat one block, but change the colors. Take another block and enlarge it to make a crib quilt. Start a block exchange with your quilty friends. Be brave and try new techniques to create a sampler quilt. What other ways can you think of to create quilts from these blocks?

Appliqué
BLOCKS

Asian Grapes

Laura Nownes • dianaandlaura.blogspot.com

MATERIALS

Appliqué patterns are on the enclosed disk.

Cream tone-on-tone fabric
   1 square, 13½" x 13½" (A)

Assorted green prints
   1 bias strip, 1½" x 32", for circle (B)
   1 *each* of patterns C–H and Q–X
   1 bias strip, 1" x 8", for stems (see "Instructions," right, to cut I, J, and K)

Assorted purple prints
   1 *each* of patterns L and O
   2 *each* of patterns M and P
   3 of pattern N

INSTRUCTIONS

1. Prepare the appliqué pieces and bias strips for turned-edge appliqué (see "Bias Strips" on page 122). Cut the narrow bias strip into 1½", 2", and 3" lengths for stems I, J, and K.

2. Fold A in half both ways and lightly crease the folds. Use the creases and the appliqué placement diagram as a guide to arrange the appliqués on A.

3. Placing the ends so they will be covered by G/H, center B and appliqué its outside perimeter to A using a blind stitch. In alphabetical order, appliqué the remaining appliqués and bias strips to A; notice that several appliqués are tucked underneath the inside perimeter of B. When all of the tucked-under pieces have been added, appliqué the inside perimeter of B. Then appliqué G/H.

4. Centering the appliqué, trim the block to 12½" x 12½".

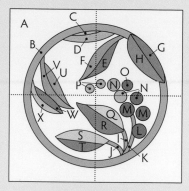

Appliqué placement

Birds and Blooms

Pearl P. Pereira • p3designs.com

MATERIALS

Appliqué patterns are on the enclosed disk.

Beige tone-on-tone fabric
   1 square, 13½" x 13½" (A)

Assorted green tone-on-tone fabrics
   1"-wide bias strips for curved stems

Assorted pink, blue, yellow, and green prints
   Appliqué pieces

Embroidery floss: Gold and black

INSTRUCTIONS

1. Cut the appliqué pieces and bias stems. Prepare the pieces for turned-edge appliqué. Refer to "Bias Strips" on page 122 to make the stems.

2. Fold A in half diagonally both ways and lightly crease the folds. Use the creases, the appliqué placement diagram, and the block photo to arrange the appliqués on A.

3. Use matching thread and a blind stitch to appliqué the pieces, starting with those that lie underneath other shapes. Use a backstitch to add antennae to the bumblebees and French knots for the birds' eyes. (Embroidery stitches are on page 126.) Add embroidery to the flowers as shown on the pattern.

4. Centering the appliqué, trim the block to 12½" x 12½".

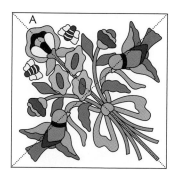

Appliqué placement

Bird's-Eye View

Dawn Heese • dawnheesequilts.blogspot.com

MATERIALS

Appliqué patterns are on the enclosed disk.

Tan dotted fabric
1 square, 13½" x 13½" (A)

Black print
1 of pattern B

2 red prints
1 of pattern C from one red print
5 of pattern D from the other red print

Green plaid
1 bias strip, 1" x 13", for stem
1 *each* of patterns D and D reversed

2 gold prints
1 of pattern D from one gold print
1 of pattern E from the other gold print

INSTRUCTIONS

1. Prepare pieces B–E for turned-edge appliqué. Make the bias stem, referring to "Bias Strips" on page 122.

2. Fold A in half both ways and lightly crease the folds. Use the creases and the appliqué placement diagram as a guide to arrange the stem and appliqués on A. Blindstitch the appliqués in place.

3. Centering the appliqué, trim the block to 12½" x 12½".

Appliqué placement

Button Basket

Ann Weber • ginghamgirls.biz

MATERIALS

Appliqué pattern is on the enclosed disk.

Light-yellow tone-on-tone fabric
1 square, 13½" x 13½" (A)

Large-scale plaid
1 of pattern B
Light-green print
1 bias strip, 1¾" x 14½", for handle
Light-green checked fabric
1 bias strip, 1½" x 11", for basket trim
Buttons: 4 red, ⅝" diameter, and 1 gold, ⅞" diameter

INSTRUCTIONS

1. Prepare the bias strips (see "Bias Strips" on page 122) and B for turned-edge appliqué.

2. Fold A in half both ways and lightly crease the folds. Use the creases and the appliqué placement diagram as a guide to arrange the basket, handle, and basket trim on A.

3. Stitch the appliqués in place.

4. Centering the appliqué, trim the block to 12½" x 12½". Sew the buttons on the basket as shown.

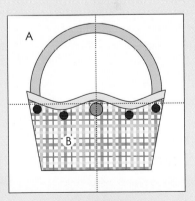

Appliqué placement

Delectable Grapes

Marian Mapes

MATERIALS

Appliqué patterns are on the enclosed disk.

Light-gold batik
1 square, 13½" x 13½" (A)

Assorted purple batiks
34 of pattern B
6 of pattern C

Dark-green batik #1
1 of pattern D

Dark-green batik #2
1 of pattern E

Medium-green batik
1 of pattern F

Light-green batik #1
1 of pattern G

Light-green batik #2
1 of pattern H

Fusible web

INSTRUCTIONS

1. Prepare the fabrics for fusible appliqué.

2. Fold A in half both ways and lightly crease the folds. Use the creases and appliqué placement diagram to arrange the pieces on A; fuse in alphabetical order. Using matching thread and a straight stitch, machine stitch close to the edges of each shape.

3. Centering the appliqué, trim the block to 12½" x 12½".

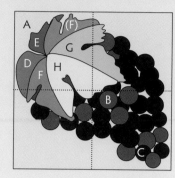

Appliqué placement

Faire la Bise

Helen Stubbings • hugsnkisses.net

MATERIALS

Appliqué patterns are on the enclosed disk.

Tan solid
1 square, 13½" x 13½" (A)

Blue print #1
4 of pattern B

Red print #1
4 of pattern C

Blue print #2
5 of pattern D
4 of pattern E

Red print #2
4 of pattern F

Embroidery floss: Red and medium blue

INSTRUCTIONS

1. Prepare pieces B–E for turned-edge appliqué.

2. Fold A in half both ways and lightly crease the folds. Use the creases and the appliqué placement diagram as a guide to arrange the B, C, center D, and E pieces on A. Hand stitch these appliqués in place.

3. Centering the appliqué, trim the block to 12½" x 12½".

4. Prepare the curved edges of the F pieces for turned-edge appliqué. Stitch an F and D to each corner of the block.

5. Use a stem stitch and lazy daisy stitch (see page 126) to add the embroidery. Notice that each lazy daisy on F is doubled and the red lazy daisy stitches on A encircle a blue straight stitch.

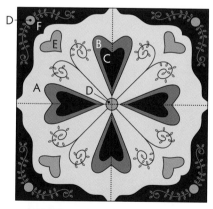

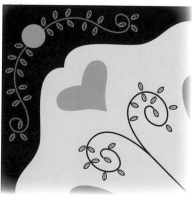

Embroidery detail

Flower Box

Kathy York • aquamoonartquilts.blogspot.com

MATERIALS

Appliqué patterns are on the enclosed disk.

Blue solid
1 square, 13½" x 13½" (A)

Assorted prints and solids
4 of pattern B
4 of pattern C
4 *each* of patterns D and D reversed
4 of pattern E
4 of pattern F
4 of pattern G
1 of pattern H
Fusible web

INSTRUCTIONS

Kathy fussy cut pieces from her fabric; if you want to replicate the white dots in the center square, consider adding buttons.

1. Prepare pieces B–H for fusible appliqué.

2. Fold A in half both ways and lightly crease the folds. Use the creases and the appliqué placement diagram as a guide to arrange the appliqués on A. Fuse them in place in alphabetical order.

3. Use matching thread to machine satin stitch around all the pieces.

4. Centering the appliqué, trim the block to 12½" x 12½".

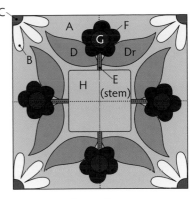

Appliqué placement

Hearts Bejeweled

Susan Guzman • suzguzdesigns.com

MATERIALS

Appliqué patterns are on the enclosed disk.

White dotted fabric
1 square, 13½" x 13½" (A)

Brown dotted fabric
1 square, 1¼" x 1¼" (B)
12 of pattern G
Yellow print
4 squares, 2" x 2" (C)
Green solid
4 rectangles, 1" x 3½" (D)
Pink tone-on-tone fabric
4 of pattern E
Blue print
4 of pattern F

INSTRUCTIONS

1. Prepare pieces B–G for turned-edge appliqué.

2. Fold A in half both ways and lightly crease the folds. Use the creases and the appliqué placement diagram as a guide to arrange the appliqués on A. Hand stitch the appliqués in place.

3. Centering the appliqué, trim the block to 12½" x 12½".

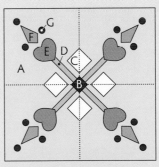

Appliqué placement

Homestead Hearts

Martha Walker • wagonswestdesigns.com

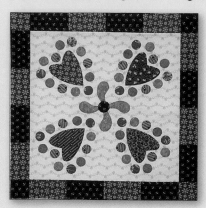

MATERIALS

Appliqué patterns are on the enclosed disk.

Cream print
    1 square, 11½" x 11½" (A)
Assorted green prints
    4 of pattern B
    48 of pattern E

Burgundy print
    1 of pattern C
    8 rectangles, 1½" x 3" (F)
    2 squares, 1½" x 1½" (G)
4 assorted medium-purple prints
    1 of pattern D from *each* fabric
        (4 total)
    8 rectangles, 1½" x 3", from one fabric
        (F)
    2 squares, 1½" x 1½", from the same
        fabric (G)

INSTRUCTIONS

1. Prepare pieces B–E for turned-edge appliqué.

2. Fold A in half diagonally both ways and lightly crease the folds. Use the creases and the appliqué placement diagram as a guide to arrange the appliqués on A. Hand stitch in place.

3. Centering the appliqué, trim the block to 10½" x 10½".

4. Sew the F and G pieces to A as shown to complete the block.

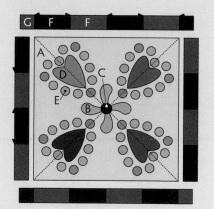

Appliqué placement
and block piecing

Hope Blooms

Nancy Halvorsen • arttoheart.com

MATERIALS

Appliqué patterns are on the enclosed disk.

Cream tone-on-tone fabric
    1 square, 12½" x 12½" (A)
Green tone-on-tone fabric
    4 squares, 4½" x 4½" (B)
Assorted blue, green, red, yellow, and pink prints
    1 set of appliqué pieces

Fusible web
Embroidery floss: Colors to match appliqués

INSTRUCTIONS

1. Referring, to the "Stitch and Flip" technique on page 124, add the B pieces to the corners of A.

2. Prepare the appliqué pieces for fusible appliqué.

3. Fold A in half both ways and lightly crease the folds. Use the creases and the appliqué placement diagram as a guide to arrange the appliqués on A. Mark the placement of the embroidered words.

4. Fuse the heart/stem pieces in place. Use matching thread and a machine blanket stitch to sew around each piece. Repeat the process for the flower and leaf pieces.

5. Use three strands of embroidery floss and a backstitch (see page 126) to hand embroider the words.

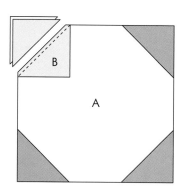

Block piecing

Appliqué placement

How About a Kiss?

Heidi Pridemore • thewhimsicalworkshop.com

MATERIALS

Appliqué patterns are on the enclosed disk.

Blue tone-on-tone fabric
1 square, 13½" x 13½" (A)

Assorted tone-on-tone fabrics
1 *each* of patterns B–J and N–T
(add ½" to all outside edges of T)

White solid
2 of pattern L

Black solid
1 of pattern K
2 of pattern M

Fusible web

INSTRUCTIONS

1. Fold A in half both ways and lightly crease the folds.

2. Prepare pieces B–S for fusible appliqué. Prepare piece T for turned-edge appliqué.

3. Use the creases and the appliqué placement diagram as a guide to arrange B–S on A; fuse to A in alphabetical order. Use black thread and a blanket stitch to machine stitch around all of the pieces.

4. Appliqué T to A using a blind stitch and matching or invisible thread.

5. Centering the appliqué, trim the block to 12½" x 12½".

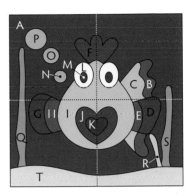

Appliqué placement

Hummingbird Haven

Cathy Van Bruggen • cathyvb.com

MATERIALS

Appliqué patterns are on the enclosed disk.

Light-green tone-on-tone fabric
1 square, 13½" x 13½" (A)

Brown tone-on-tone fabric
1 bias strip, ¾" x 13", for stem

Assorted tone-on-tone fabrics
1 set of leaf pieces
1 *each* of patterns B–R
2 bias strips, 2" x 3", for flower blossoms

Embroidery floss: Light-gray, fuchsia, green
Seed beads: 12 pink
Brown Micron Pigma pen

INSTRUCTIONS

1. Referring to "Narrow Bias Stems" on page 123, prepare the brown bias strip and appliqué pieces for turned-edge appliqué.

2. Fold A in half both ways and lightly crease the folds. Use the creases and appliqué placement diagram to arrange the stem on A. Use a stem stitch to embroider the end of the bias strip, the small stem, and the "ground" line as shown. (See "Embroidery Stitches" on page 126.)

3. Arrange the leaves and pieces B–D, G–I, and L–R on A. Hand stitch the leaves and other appliqués in alphabetical order.

4. For each blossom, fold a bias strip in half lengthwise, wrong sides together. Sew a running stitch ⅛" from the edge.

Gather the stitching as shown. Baste the blossoms to B and G. Add appliqués E, F, J, and K.

5. Use beads and embroidery floss in a combination of satin, outline, couching, and stem stitches to add the details and the spiderweb (see diagram below). Draw the hummingbird's feet and underbelly using the brown pen.

6. Centering the appliqué, trim the block to 12½" x 12½".

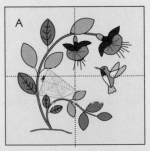

Appliqué and embroidery placement

Hungry

Terry Clothier Thompson • terrythompson.com

MATERIALS

Appliqué patterns are on the enclosed disk.

Cream print
1 square, 13½" x 13½" (A)

Assorted green prints
1 *each* of patterns B and H
2 of pattern D
3 of pattern F

Large-scale multicolored print
1 of pattern C

Black print
1 of pattern E

Yellow print
6 of pattern F
1 of pattern I

Red tone-on-tone fabric
1 of pattern G

INSTRUCTIONS

1. Prepare pieces B–I for turned-edge appliqué.

2. Fold A in half both ways and lightly crease the folds. Use the creases and the appliqué placement diagram as a guide to arrange the pieces on A. Stitch the pieces in place in alphabetical order using a tiny machine zigzag stitch.

3. Centering the appliqué, trim the block to 12½" x 12½".

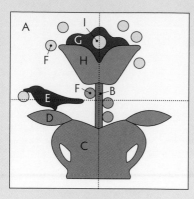

Appliqué placement

Isabelle

Lynda Howell • stitchconnection.com

MATERIALS

Appliqué patterns are on the enclosed disk.

Blue tone-on-tone fabric
1 square, 11½" x 11½" (A)

Gray tone-on-tone fabric
1 of pattern B (add ½" to all straight outside edges)

Assorted red, blue, green, gold, and brown prints
1 *each* of patterns C, F, H–N, and P–W
2 of pattern D

White felt
1 *each* of patterns E and O
2 of pattern G

Red tone-on-tone fabric
1 rectangle, 1½" x 10½" (X)
1 rectangle, 1½" x 11½" (Y)

Green-checked fabric
1 rectangle, 1½" x 11½" (Y)
1 rectangle, 1½" x 12½" (Z)

Embroidery floss: Black and blue
Fusible web
Acrylic paint for cheeks

INSTRUCTIONS

1. Prepare pieces B–W for fusible appliqué. Refer to the appliqué placement diagram and arrange the pieces in alphabetical order on A. Before fusing, tuck pieces of blue floss under the ends of the scarf (L and M) to create fringe. Fuse the pieces in place.

2. Using matching thread and a machine blanket stitch or other decorative stitches, sew around all of the appliqués.

3. By hand, satin stitch the eyes and backstitch the mouth (see "Embroidery Stitches" on page 126). Add color to the cheeks using the acrylic paint and a dry brush or powder blush.

4. Centering the appliqué, trim the block to 10½" x 10½". Add pieces X–Z as shown to complete the block.

Appliqué placement
and block piecing

Lillebet's Bouquet

Beth Ferrier • applewoodfarmquilts.com

MATERIALS

Appliqué patterns are on the enclosed disk.

Off-white tone-on-tone fabric
1 square, 13½" x 13½" (A)

Assorted green tone-on-tone fabrics
3 of pattern B

Assorted red tone-on-tone fabrics
3 each of patterns C, D, and E

Gold tone-on-tone fabric
7 of pattern F

Assorted blue tone-on-tone fabrics*
2 each of patterns G, G reversed, and H
1 each of patterns I, I reversed, J,
J reversed, K, and L
Beth used the wrong side of one fabric for the shading on her ribbon.
Embroidery floss: Yellow
Monofilament

INSTRUCTIONS

1. Prepare pieces B–L for turned-edge appliqué.

2. Fold A in half both ways and lightly crease the folds. Use the creases and the appliqué placement diagram as a guide to arrange the appliqués on A.

3. Appliqué the pieces in place in alphabetical order using monofilament and a machine zigzag stitch. Use a variegated thread to add a straight stitch just inside the edges of the bow pieces and veins to the leaves.

4. Add detail to the flowers as shown at right using a backstitch and two or three strands of yellow embroidery floss.

5. Centering the appliqué, trim the block to 12½" x 12½".

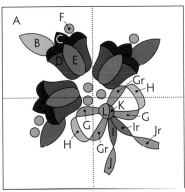

Appliqué placement

Love Apple

Jo Morton • jomortonquilts.com

MATERIALS

Appliqué patterns are on the enclosed disk.

Tan print
1 square, 13½" x 13½" (A)

Assorted green prints
2 of pattern B
4 of pattern D
8 of pattern F

Assorted red prints
4 each of patterns C and G

Assorted gold prints
4 of pattern E

INSTRUCTIONS

1. Prepare pieces B–G for turned-edge appliqué.

2. Fold A in half both ways and lightly crease the folds. Use the creases and the appliqué placement diagram as a guide to arrange the appliqués on A.

3. Use matching thread and a blind stitch to appliqué the pieces to A.

4. Centering the appliqué, trim the block to 12½" x 12½".

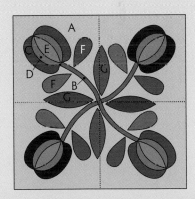

Appliqué placement

Love Bird
Marian Mapes

MATERIALS

Appliqué patterns are on the enclosed disk.

Pale-gold batik
1 square, 13½" x 13½" (A)
Brown batik
1 of pattern B

Assorted green batiks
2 of pattern C
6 of pattern C reversed
Assorted blue batiks
1 *each* of patterns D–F
Black batik
1 of pattern G
Fusible web

INSTRUCTIONS

1. Prepare pieces B-G for fusible appliqué.

2. Fold A in half both ways and lightly crease the folds. Use the creases and the appliqué placement diagram as a guide to arrange the pieces on A; fuse in alphabetical order.

3. Using matching thread and a straight stitch, sew close to the edges of each piece.

4. Centering the appliqué, trim the block to 12½" x 12½".

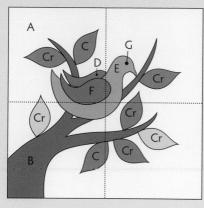

Appliqué placement

Merry Little Flower
Kari Ramsay • freshcutquilts.com

MATERIALS

Appliqué patterns are on the enclosed disk.

White tone-on-tone fabric
1 square, 13½" x 13½" (A)
Light-green print
1 *each* of patterns B and E

Red print
1 of pattern C
Black print
6 of pattern D
Yellow print
1 circle, 4" diameter, for yo-yo

INSTRUCTIONS

1. Prepare pieces B–E for turned-edge appliqué.

2. Fold A in half both ways and lightly crease the folds. Use the creases and the appliqué placement diagram as a guide to arrange the appliqués on A.

3. Use matching thread and a blind stitch to appliqué the pieces in place.

4. Refer to the yo-yo instructions on page 125 and use the 4" yellow circle to make a yo-yo. Tack the yo-yo in place at the flower's center.

5. Centering the appliqué, trim the block to 12½" x 12½".

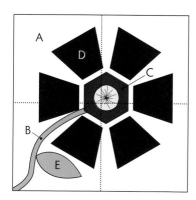

Appliqué placement

Midnight Sun Garden

Jane Quinn • quiltinginthecountry.com

MATERIALS

Appliqué patterns are on the enclosed disk.

Green tone-on-tone fabric
1 square, 13½" x 13½" (A)
Purple print
4 of pattern B

Yellow print
4 of pattern B
Green print
8 of pattern C
Red print
4 of pattern D
Fusible web
Embroidery floss: Green

INSTRUCTIONS

1. Prepare pieces B-D for fusible appliqué.

2. Fold A in half horizontally, vertically, and diagonally and lightly crease the folds. Use the creases and the appliqué placement diagram as a guide to arrange the pieces on A; fuse in alphabetical order.

3. Use the green floss and a blanket stitch (see page 126) to sew around all of the appliqués.

4. Centering the appliqué, trim the block to 12½" x 12½".

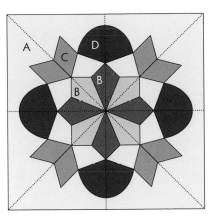

Appliqué placement

My Peony

Diana McClun • dianaandlaura.blogspot.com

MATERIALS

Appliqué patterns are on the enclosed disk.

Cream tone-on-tone fabric
1 square, 13½" x 13½" (A)
Assorted green prints
1 bias strip, 1" x 11", for stem (B)
1 each of patterns L–R

Assorted blue and purple prints
1 *each* of patterns C–K
Fusible web

INSTRUCTIONS

1. Refer to "Bias Strips" on page 122 to prepare the bias strip for turned-edge appliqué. Prepare pieces C–R for fusible appliqué.

2. Fold A in half both ways and lightly crease the folds. Use the creases and the appliqué placement diagram as a guide to arrange the appliqués on A.

3. Curving it casually, appliqué bias strip B (stem) to A with a blind stitch. Fuse the remaining pieces in alphabetical order. Machine stitch around the pieces with a blanket stitch.

4. Centering the appliqué, trim the block to 12½" x 12½".

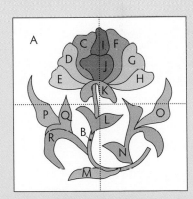

Appliqué placement

19

Norse Bloom

Karen Comstock • quiltricks.com

MATERIALS

Appliqué patterns are on the enclosed disk.

Cream tone-on-tone fabric
1 square, 13½" x 13½" (A)

Green tone-on-tone fabric
1 bias strip, 1" x 20", for stems
1 set of leaf pieces

Dark-pink tone-on-tone fabric
3 circles, 2" diameter, for rosebuds

Medium-pink tone-on-tone fabric
1 *each* of patterns B–E

Fusible web
Embroidery floss: Brown, green, and dark pink

INSTRUCTIONS

1. Refer to "Bias Strips" (page 122) to make the stems. Cut one stem 12¼" long and one stem 7¾" long. Prepare the leaves and flower petals (B–E) and leaves (F–S) for fusible appliqué.

2. Fold A in half both ways and lightly crease the folds. Use the creases and the appliqué placement diagram to arrange the stems on A. Use matching thread and a blind stitch to appliqué the stems in place.

3. Arrange and fuse B to A. Use matching thread and a machine blanket stitch to sew around the pieces.

4. To make a folded rosebud, fold a dark-pink circle in half, wrong sides together, and then fold the sides as shown. Make three folded rosebuds. Use a running stitch along the bottom of each one to secure to A at the end of

the stems as shown and on the B piece. Fuse pieces C–S and the leaves as shown.

Rosebud folding

5. Use a backstitch, lazy daisy stitch, and French knots to add details as shown (see "Embroidery Stitches" on page 126).

6. Centering the appliqué, trim the block to 12½" x 12½".

Appliqué and embroidery placement

Nucleus

Scarlett Rose • scarlettrose.com

MATERIALS

Appliqué patterns are on the enclosed disk.

Medium-teal batik
1 square, 13½" x 13½" (A)

Pale-yellow batik
1 of pattern B

Light-blue tone-on-tone fabric
1 of pattern C

Dark-teal tone-on-tone fabric
1 bias strip, 1¼" x 82"*

Mauve tone-on-tone fabric
1 bias strip, 1¼" x 31½"*

Optional: Clover ⅜" fusible bias-tape maker and 5 mm fusible web

***Note:** Scarlett used a fusible bias-tape maker and fusible web to prepare her bias strips. If you prefer this method, follow the manufacturer's instructions for cutting the bias strips.

INSTRUCTIONS

1. Fold A in half both ways and lightly crease the folds. Use the creases and the appliqué placement diagram as a guide to center B on A. Baste B in place around the outer edges and cut away the excess A under the appliqué. Repeat to add C and cut away the excess B.

2. Refer to "Bias Strips" on page 122 to prepare the two bias strips. Place the bias strips on A, covering the raw edges of B and C; refer to the diagram and note that some strips overlap others and some underlap. Fold the teal strip at the

outer corners. Use matching thread and a machine blind stitch to sew the strips in place.

3. Centering the appliqué, trim the block to 12½" x 12½".

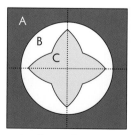

Appliqué placement

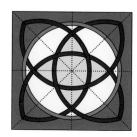

Bias-strip placement

One Happy Family

Kathy Patterson • mccallsquilting.com

MATERIALS

Appliqué patterns are on the enclosed disk.

Cream toile
1 square, 13½" x 13½" (A)

Purple tone-on-tone fabric
3 of pattern B
Pink tone-on-tone fabric
1 of pattern B
Assorted green prints
20 of pattern C
Gold tone-on-tone fabric
4 of pattern D
Fusible web
Metallic thread: Gold

INSTRUCTIONS

1. Prepare pieces B–N for fusible appliqué. Arrange the appliqués on A as shown and fuse in place. Using gold metallic thread, machine blanket-stitch around the pieces.

2. Centering the appliqué, trim the block to 12½" x 12½".

Appliqué placement

Paisley Punch

Diane Harris • quiltmaker.com

MATERIALS

Appliqué patterns are on the enclosed disk.

Aqua print
1 square, 13½" x 13½" (A)

Assorted prints and batiks
1 *each* of patterns B, D, D reversed, and E
2 *each* of patterns C and F

INSTRUCTIONS

1. Prepare pieces B–F for turned-edge appliqué.

2. Fold A in half both ways and lightly crease the folds. Use the creases and the appliqué placement diagram as a guide to arrange the pieces on A. Use matching thread and a blind stitch to appliqué the pieces in place.

3. Centering the appliqué, trim the block to 12½" x 12½".

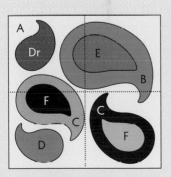

Appliqué placement

Patriotic Pinwheel

Susan McDermott • windhamfabrics.com

MATERIALS

Appliqué patterns are on the enclosed disk.

Tan print
   1 square, 13½" x 13½" (A)
Brown print
   4 of pattern B
Red-striped fabric
   4 of pattern C
Dark-blue print
   4 of pattern D
Dark-blue print
   1 of pattern E
Dark-tan print
   1 of pattern F
Red print
   1 of pattern G
Monofilament
Fusible web

INSTRUCTIONS

1. Prepare pieces B–G for fusible appliqué.

2. Fold A in half diagonally both ways and lightly crease the folds. Use the creases and the appliqué placement diagram as a guide to arrange the appliqués on A; fuse in place. Then use monofilament and a tiny zigzag stitch to sew around all the pieces.

3. Centering the appliqué, trim the block to 12½" x 12½".

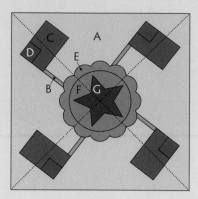

Appliqué placement

Rising Star 1

Reeze L. Hanson • morningglorydesigns.net

MATERIALS

Appliqué patterns are on the enclosed disk.

Purple mottled batik
   1 square, 12½" x 12½" (A)
Lime-green batik
   1 of pattern B
Gold dotted batik
   4 *each* of patterns C, D, E, and G
Blue-print batik
   4 *each* of patterns C, D, and F
Dark-green tone-on-tone fabric
   4 *each* of patterns C, D, and E
Fusible web
Tear-away stabilizer

INSTRUCTIONS

1. Prepare pieces B–G for fusible appliqué.

2. Fold A in half both ways and lightly crease the folds. Use the creases and the appliqué placement diagram as a guide to arrange the pieces on A, beginning with the outside pieces and working toward the center of the block. Fuse the appliqués to A.

3. Using tear-away stabilizer behind the block, sew around the pieces with gold thread and a machine blanket stitch. Remove the excess stabilizer.

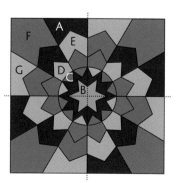

Appliqué placement

Rising Star 2

Toni Kay Steere and Jenny Foltz • wingandaprayerdesign.com

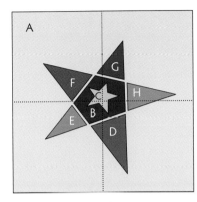

INSTRUCTIONS

1. Prepare pieces B–H for fusible appliqué.

2. Fold A in half both ways and lightly crease the folds. Use the creases and the appliqué placement diagram as a guide to arrange the pieces on A; fuse in place.

3. Using thread to match each piece, machine blanket-stitch around the pieces.

4. Use a stem stitch (see page 126) to embroider the curved lines. Centering the appliqué, trim the block to 12½" x 12½".

5. Referring to the detail photo above right and "Beading," on page 125, add beads as desired and stack several buttons at the center of the small star; sew in place.

Appliqué placement

MATERIALS

Appliqué patterns are on the enclosed disk.

Beige tone-on-tone fabric
1 square, 13½" x 13½" (A)
Assorted tone-on-tone fabrics
1 *each* of patterns B–H
Fusible web
Beads and buttons as desired
Embroidery floss: Red, green, purple, and gold

Rosie's Posie

Cara Bonner • thequiltnook.com

MATERIALS

Yo-yo patterns are on the enclosed disk.

Cream print
1 square, 13½" x 13½" (A)
Green print
3 bias strips, 1¼" x 8¼", for stems
Assorted red, brown, tan, and cream prints
3 circles, 5" diameter, for large yo-yos

11 circles, 4" diameter, for medium yo-yos
8 circles, 2¾" diameter, for small yo-yos
Rickrack: 21" length of narrow white
Embroidery floss: Light green
Optional: Clover small, large, and extra-large yo-yo makers

INSTRUCTIONS

1. Refer to "Bias Strips" on page 122 to make stems from the bias strips. Refer to the yo-yo instructions on page 125 to make yo-yos using the assorted circles.

2. Fold A in half both ways and lightly crease the folds. Use the creases and the appliqué placement diagram as a guide to arrange the stems on A. Tuck the white rickrack under the stems. Using a contrasting thread and a machine blanket stitch, sew around the stems.

3. Referring to the placement diagram, arrange the large yo-yos on A; tack them in place. Repeat with the medium yo-yos, followed by the small yo-yos.

4. Refer to "Embroidery Stitches" on page 126 to hand embroider tendrils and small stems using a stem stitch as shown. Stitch French knots randomly. Tie the rickrack in a bow around the stems to complete the bouquet.

5. Centering the appliqué, trim the block to 12½" x 12½".

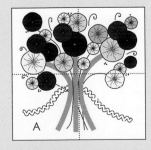

Appliqué and embroidery placement

Seven Eighths

Vicki Willems

MATERIALS

Appliqué patterns are on the enclosed disk.

Cream batik
1 square, 13½" x 13½" (A)

Assorted red, orange, and gold batiks
1 *each* of patterns B and D
7 *each* of patterns H, I, and J

Blue batik
1 of pattern C

Assorted green batiks
7 *each* of patterns E, F, and G

Monofilament

Fusible web

INSTRUCTIONS

1. Prepare pieces B–J for fusible appliqué.

2. Fold A in half both ways and lightly crease the folds. Use the creases and the appliqué placement diagram as a guide to arrange the appliqués on A. Fuse the appliqués to A in alphabetical order.

3. Use monofilament and a machine zigzag stitch to sew around the pieces.

4. Centering the appliqué, trim the block to 12½" x 12½".

Appliqué placement

Simply Sweet

Barbara Jones • quiltsoup.com

MATERIALS

Appliqué patterns are on the enclosed disk.

White dotted fabric
1 square, 13½" x 13½" (A)

Green print #1
1 *each* of patterns B and C

Green print #2
1 of pattern B

Red print
1 of pattern D

Blue print
1 of pattern E

White print
1 of pattern F

Buttons: 1 flower, 1⅛" diameter, and 1 round, ½" diameter

INSTRUCTIONS

1. Prepare pieces B–F for turned-edge appliqué.

2. Fold A in half both ways and lightly crease the folds. Use the creases and the appliqué placement diagram as a guide to arrange the appliqués on A. Use matching thread to hand stitch the appliqués in place.

3. Centering the appliqué, trim the block to 12½" x 12½".

4. Add the ½" button for the bird's eye and the flower button at the top of the flower as shown, referring to the block photo for placement.

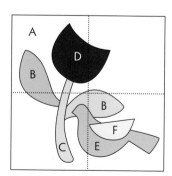

Appliqué placement

Snow Happy Home

Monica Solorio-Snow • thehappyzombie.com

MATERIALS

Appliqué patterns are on the enclosed disk.

Yellow dotted fabric
1 square, 13½" x 13½" (A)
Light-blue print
1 of pattern B
White print
1 of pattern D

Tan print
1 *each* of patterns C and H
Assorted red prints
1 *each* of patterns E, G, and L–N
Yellow print
1 of pattern F
Assorted green prints
1 *each* of patterns I–K
Buttons: ⅝" and ½" diameter (for doorknob)

INSTRUCTIONS

1. Prepare pieces B–N for turned-edge appliqué.

2. Fold A in half both ways and lightly crease the folds. Use the creases and the appliqué placement diagram as a guide to arrange the appliqués on A.

3. Use matching thread and a blind stitch to appliqué the pieces in alphabetical order.

4. Centering the appliqué, trim the block to 12½" x 12½".

5. Stack the small button on top of the larger button and sew them to the block for a doorknob.

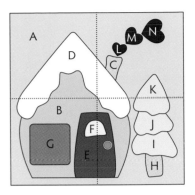

Appliqué placement

Snowman Farm

June Dudley • quiltmaker.com

MATERIALS

Appliqué patterns are on the enclosed disk.

Blue batik
1 square, 13" x 13" (A)
3 assorted green batiks
1 strip, 5½" x 13", from *each* fabric
White-on-white print
1 strip, 5½" x 13"
Legal-sized paper, 2 sheets
Fusible web
Chalk pen fabric marker

INSTRUCTIONS

1. The trees and snowmen are cut from patterns that you make like a paper doll. Fold a 5½" x 12" strip of paper in half and then accordian fold to measure 5½" x 1½". Trace the trees (B) onto the top panel of the folded paper. Cut on the traced lines through all layers. Repeat to make the snowmen (C).

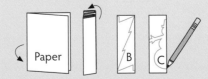

2. Unfold the patterns. Center and trace both tree rows onto a 5½" x 13" strip of fusible web as shown, adding the line shown in red to each end. Repeat to trace an additional row of trees and one row of snowmen. Fuse a set of trees to each green strip. Fuse the snowmen

to the white strip. Carefully cut on the drawn lines.

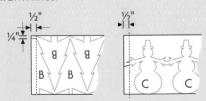

Fusible-web placement

3. Mark A as shown. Center the first row of trees on the top line; fuse in place. Use matching thread to stitch close to the appliqué edges. Repeat for the remaining rows, offsetting them as shown.

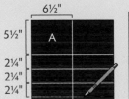

4. Center and trim the block to 12½" x 12½".

25

Southern Blooms

Pat Wys • silverthimblequilt.com

MATERIALS

Appliqué patterns are on the enclosed disk.

Assorted cream prints
4 squares, 7½" x 7½" (A)
Assorted green prints
8 bias strips, ⅞" x 5", for stems
16 of pattern B
Assorted red prints
8 of pattern C

Assorted gold prints
8 of pattern D
Buttons: 8 small brown

INSTRUCTIONS

The block is made from four units. The appliqué placement is casual; each unit is different. When placing the appliqué, keep in mind where the seam allowance will be once the unit is trimmed, leaving space between the flowers and the seam allowance.

1. Prepare the bias strips and pieces B–D for turned-edge appliqué. Using a hand or machine blanket stitch (see page 126), appliqué two bias strips (stems) to each A square, followed by pieces B–D in alphabetical order, as shown.

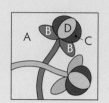

Appliqué placement

2. Centering the appliqué, trim each unit to 6½" x 6½".

3. Join the sections as shown to make the block. Sew a button to each flower.

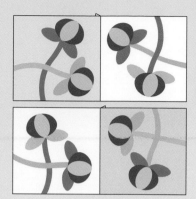

Block piecing

Spring Flowers

Lynda Milligan and Nancy Smith • possibilitiesquilt.com

MATERIALS

Appliqué patterns are on the enclosed disk.

Dark-blue batik
1 square, 13½" x 13½" (A)
Assorted green batiks
1 *each* of patterns B–D, I, J, M, N, P,
P reversed, and Q
2 of pattern O

Assorted pink and orange batiks
1 *each* of patterns E, G, H, K, and L
3 of pattern F
2 *each* of patterns R–T
Fusible web
Nonstick pressing sheet

INSTRUCTIONS

1. Prepare pieces B–T for fusible appliqué.

2. Fold A in half both ways and lightly crease the folds. Lay the nonstick pressing sheet on a hard ironing surface. Using the appliqué placement diagram as a guide, lightly fuse pieces B–T in alphabetical order to the pressing sheet. Let the pieces cool, peel off as a unit, and position to the background as shown, using the creases as a guide. Fuse in place.

3. Use matching thread and a machine blanket stitch to sew around all of the appliqués.

4. Centering the appliqué, trim the block to 12½" x 12½".

Appliqué placement

Spring Snowflake

Kathy K. Wylie • kathykwylie.com

MATERIALS

Appliqué patterns are on the enclosed disk.

White-on-white print
  1 square, 13½" x 13½" (A)

Green tone-on-tone fabric
  1 of pattern B

Pink tone-on-tone fabric
  6 of pattern C

INSTRUCTIONS

1. Prepare pieces B and C for turned-edge appliqué (B will need to be flipped to trace the whole pattern).

2. Fold A in half both ways and lightly crease the folds. Use the creases and the appliqué placement diagram as a guide to arrange the pieces on A. Use matching thread and a blind stitch to appliqué the pieces in place.

3. Centering the appliqué, trim the block to 12½" x 12½".

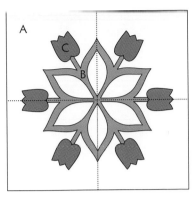

Appliqué placement

Summer Pop

Pat Sloan • patsloan.com

MATERIALS

Appliqué patterns are on the enclosed disk.

Gold print
  1 square, 13½" x 13½" (A)

Green print #1
  1 of pattern B
  4 of pattern F

Green print #2
  1 of pattern C
  4 of pattern G

Red print
  1 of pattern D

Pink print
  3 of pattern E

Black print
  1 of pattern F

Pink tone-on-tone fabric
  1 of pattern G

Fusible web

INSTRUCTIONS

1. Prepare pieces B–G for fusible appliqué.

2. Fold A in half both ways and lightly crease the folds. Use the creases and the appliqué placement diagram as a guide to arrange the pieces on A; fuse in alphabetical order.

3. Use matching thread and a machine blanket stitch to sew around the pieces.

4. Centering the appliqué, trim the block to 12½" x 12½".

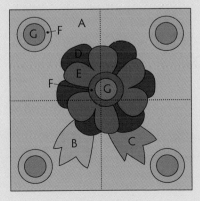

Appliqué placement

Uncle Sam's Hat

Laurie Simpson • minickandsimpson.com

MATERIALS

Appliqué patterns are on the enclosed disk.

Cream-striped fabric
1 square, 13½" x 13½" (A)

Green tone-on-tone fabric
1 bias strip, 1" x 11", for stems

Assorted red, cream, and blue prints and tone-on-tone fabrics
1 *each* of patterns B–C reversed and H–M
3 *each* of patterns D, E, and G
2 of pattern F

Brown tone-on-tone fabric
1 bias strip, 1" x 6½", for flagpole

INSTRUCTIONS

1. Prepare pieces B–M for turned-edge appliqué.

2. To make the bias stems, refer to "Bias Strips" on page 122. Cut the green bias strip into smaller strips as shown on the full-sized block pattern on the disk.

3. Fold A in half diagonally both ways and lightly crease the folds. Use the creases and appliqué placement diagram as a guide to arrange the pieces and bias strips on A. Use matching thread to hand stitch the appliqués in place.

4. Centering the appliqué, trim the block to 12½" x 12½".

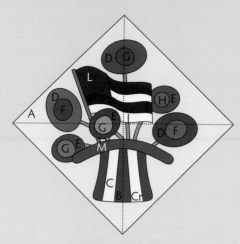

Appliqué placement

Watering Can

Kay Mackenzie • quiltpuppy.com; allaboutapplique.net

MATERIALS

Appliqué patterns are on the enclosed disk.

Off-white tone-on-tone fabric
1 square, 13½" x 13½" (A)

Blue print
1 *each* of patterns B, C, and E

Blue-checked fabric
1 of pattern D

Green tone-on-tone fabric
2 of pattern F
1 *each* of patterns H–I reversed

Red print
1 *each* of patterns G and K

Gold print
1 of pattern J

INSTRUCTIONS

1. Prepare pieces B–K for turned-edge appliqué.

2. Fold A in half both ways and lightly crease the folds. Use the creases and the appliqué placement diagram as a guide to arrange the pieces on A. Use matching thread to hand stitch the appliqués in place.

3. Centering the appliqué, trim the block to 12½" x 12½".

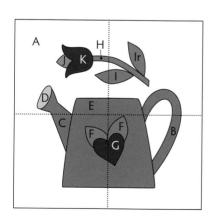

Appliqué placement

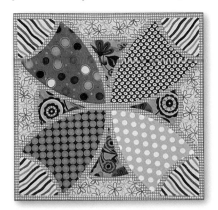

Winding New Ways

Bobbi Finley and Carol Gilham Jones

MATERIALS

Appliqué patterns are on the enclosed disk.

Orange-checked fabric
   1 square, 13½" x 13½" (A)

4 assorted dot prints
   1 of pattern B from *each* fabric
      (4 total)
Multicolored striped fabric
   4 of pattern C
Cream print
   4 of pattern D
Gold print
   4 of pattern E

INSTRUCTIONS

1. Prepare pieces B–E for turned-edge appliqué.

2. Fold A in half both ways and lightly crease the folds. Use the creases and the appliqué placement diagram as a guide to arrange the pieces on A.

3. Hand stitch the appliqués in place.

4. Centering the appliqué, trim the block to 12½" x 12½".

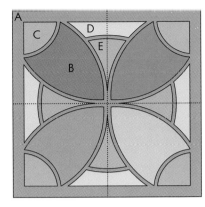

Appliqué placement

Wish You Were Here

Joni Pike • sewspecialdesigns.com

MATERIALS

Appliqué patterns are on the enclosed disk.

Olive-green print
   1 square, 12½" x 12½" (A)
Aqua tone-on-tone fabric
   1 rectangle, 6½" x 9½" (B)

Off-white tone-on-tone fabric
   1 of pattern C (add ½" to the outside edges)
Assorted prints and solids
   1 *each* of patterns D, E, and G–I
   2 of pattern F
Fusible web
Buttons and beads: ¾"-diameter button and 13 aqua seed beads
Black Pigma Micron pen

INSTRUCTIONS

1. Use a satin stitch to sew C to B. Prepare pieces D–I for fusible appliqué. Refer to the appliqué placement diagram to fuse D–I to B.

2. Use brown thread to machine blanket-stitch around the tree (D and E), chairs (F), and umbrella (H). Use brown thread and a satin stitch to sew around the umbrella pole (G) and stamp (I). Add legs to the chairs with a satin stitch.

3. Iron fusible web to the wrong side of B. Centering the design, trim B to 6" x 9". Fuse B to A as shown. Use orange thread and a satin stitch to sew around the edges. Add a button to the stamp and seed beads to the umbrella as shown on the pattern. Use the pen to add a "postmark" to the postcard.

Appliqué placement

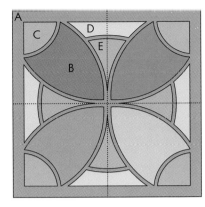

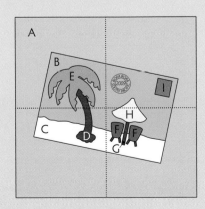

APPLIQUÉ

Pieced
BLOCKS

Ahoy
Carolyn Goins • cpgdesigns.com

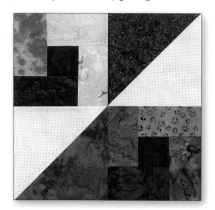

MATERIALS

▢ = Cut in half diagonally.

Brown batik
2 squares, 2½" x 2½" (A)

Assorted-color batiks
8 rectangles, 2½" x 4½" (B)
2 squares, 6⅞" x 6⅞" ▢ (C)
(You'll have 2 extra triangles.)

Light-gray batik
1 square, 6⅞" x 6⅞" ▢ (C)

INSTRUCTIONS

1. Sew a B rectangle to the bottom edge of an A square with a partial seam as shown. Sew another B to the right, to the top, and to the left of A. Then complete the partial seam. Repeat using the remaining A and B pieces.

● – Partial seam

2. Join an assorted-color batik C triangle to each light-gray C triangle.

3. Complete the block as shown.

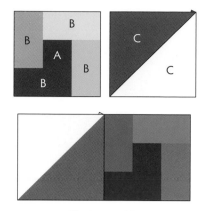

Block assembly

A-Maze-Ment
Sue Beevers

MATERIALS

▢ = Cut in half diagonally.

Beige print
10 squares, 1½" x 1½" (A)
4 rectangles, 1½" x 2½" (B)
2 rectangles, 1½" x 3½" (C)
2 rectangles, 1¼" x 1½" (F)
4 rectangles, 1½" x 4½" (G)
1 square, 2⅝" x 2⅝" ▢ (I)
2 squares, 4⅝" x 4⅝" ▢ (J)

Light-green print and blue print
3 squares, 1½" x 1½", from *each* fabric (A)
1 rectangle, 1½" x 2½", from *each* fabric (B)
2 rectangles, 1½" x 3½", from *each* fabric (C)
1 rectangle, 1½" x 5¼", from *each* fabric (H)

Dark-green print
2 rectangles, 1½" x 3½" (C)
2 rectangles, 1½" x 5¼" (H)

Red print
2 rectangles, 1¼" x 3½" (D)
4 rectangles, 1¼" x 4¼" (E)
6 rectangles, 1¼" x 1½" (F)

Gold print
1 rectangle, 1½" x 3½" (C)
2 rectangles, 1½" x 6¾" (K)

INSTRUCTIONS

1. Join the pieces as shown at right. Note that the pieces along the top and bottom will extend beyond the perimeter of the block.

2. Use contrasting thread and decorative machine stitches to embellish the green, gold, and red pieces as shown in the photo. You can preserve the block's woven effect by ending the stitching whenever one color appears to weave under another color.

3. Centering the design, trim the block to 12½" x 12½".

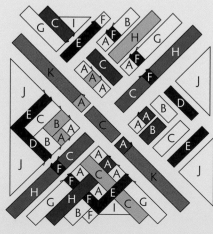

Block assembly

America the Beautiful

Paula Barnes • bonniebluequilts.com

MATERIALS

Tan print
4 squares, 2⅜" x 2⅜" (A)
16 squares, 2" x 2" (B)
8 rectangles, 2" x 3½" (C)

Navy print
4 squares, 2⅜" x 2⅜" (A)
8 squares, 2" x 2" (B)

Red print
8 rectangles, 2" x 3½" (C)

Novelty print (eagle)
1 square, 6½" x 6½" (D)*

Paula fussy cut the D piece from the novelty print to center the eagle motif.

INSTRUCTIONS

1. Refer to "Triangle Squares" on page 124. Use the tan and navy A squares to make eight of unit 1.

Unit 1.
Make 8.

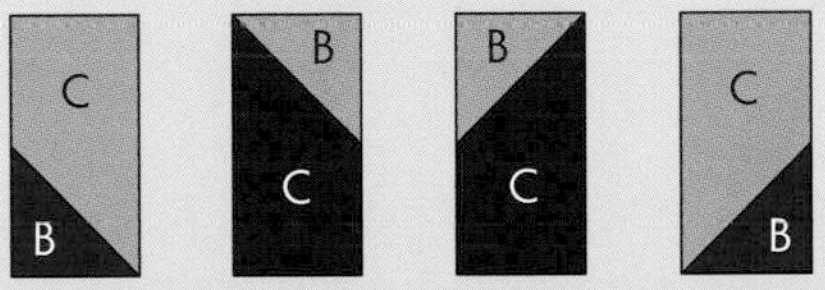

Unit 2. Unit 3. Unit 4. Unit 5.
Make 4. Make 4. Make 4. Make 4.

2. Refer to "Stitch and Flip" on page 124. Use the navy and tan B squares and the tan and red C rectangles to make units 2–5 as shown.

3. Join the units and pieces to complete the block.

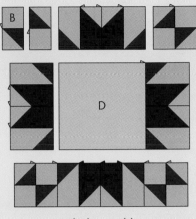

Block assembly

Antique Aster

Deborah Borsos • ppnq.com

MATERIALS

◻ = *Cut in half diagonally.*
◻ = *Cut into quarters diagonally.*

Pink print
2 squares, 1⅞" x 1⅞" (A)
4 rectangles, 1½" x 10½" (H)

Large-scale brown print
2 squares, 1⅞" x 1⅞" (A)
2 squares, 4⅞" x 4⅞" ◻ (F)
2 squares, 2¼" x 2¼" (I)

Cream print
2 squares, 2⅞" x 2⅞" (B)

2 squares, 2⅞" x 2⅞" ◻ (C)
1 square, 3¼" x 3¼" ◻ (D)
4 squares, 2½" x 2½" (G)

Burgundy print #1
2 squares, 2⅞" x 2⅞" (B)

Burgundy print #2
1 square, 3¼" x 3¼" (D)
2 squares, 2¼" x 2¼" (I)

Small-scale brown print
1 square, 5¼" x 5¼" ◻ (E)

INSTRUCTIONS

1. Use the "Triangle Squares" technique on page 124. Pair the pink and brown A squares to make four of unit 1. Pair the cream and burgundy B squares to make four of unit 2. Refer to "Quarter-Square Triangles" on page 124; use the brown and burgundy #1 squares to make four of unit 3. Sew all four of unit 1 together to make a pinwheel.

2. Sew a unit 2 and pieces C–G together to make a petal section. Make four.

Petal section.
Make 4.

3. Sew a petal section to the left side of the pinwheel with a partial seam as shown. Sew the remaining petal sections to the top, right, and bottom of the pinwheel. Complete the partial seam.

4. Sew an H rectangle to each side of the block. Add a unit 3 to each end of the two remaining H rectangles; sew these strips to the top and bottom to complete the block.

Unit 1. Unit 2. Unit 3. Pinwheel.
Make 4. Make 4. Make 4. Make 1.

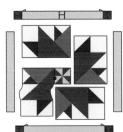

Block assembly
● = Partial seam

33

Around the Rosie

Monica Solorio-Snow • thehappyzombie.com

MATERIALS

Cream print
   1 square, 5¼" x 5¼" (A)
Green print #1
   4 squares, 2⅞" x 2⅞" (B)
Cream solid
   2 squares, 4⅞" x 4⅞" (C)
   4 rectangles, 2½" x 4½" (D)

Green print #2
   2 squares, 4⅞" x 4⅞" (C)
Large-scale floral print
   1 square, 4½" x 4½" (E)

INSTRUCTIONS

1. Refer to "Fast Flying Geese" and "Triangle Squares" on page 124. Use the cream A and green B squares to make four flying-geese units. Pair the cream and green C squares to make four triangle-square units.

Flying-geese unit.
Make 4.

Triangle-square unit.
Make 4.

2. Sew the units and D and E pieces together as shown to complete the block.

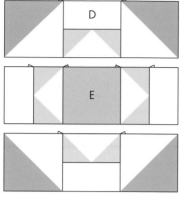

Block assembly

Bar Code

Bill Kerr and Weeks Ringle • funquilts.com

MATERIALS

Assorted blue, green, and purple solids
   About 45 strips, ¾" to 1½" wide x 7"
Pale-green solid
   2 strips, ¾" x 6⅜" (A)
   1 strip, ¾" x 12½" (B)

INSTRUCTIONS

1. Join the strips randomly to make a unit about 7" x 7". Trim the unit to 6⅜" x 6⅜". Repeat to make a total of four units.

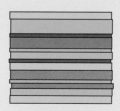

Unit piecing.
Make 4.

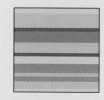

Trim to 6⅜" x 6⅜".

2. Join the units with strips A and B as shown to complete the block.

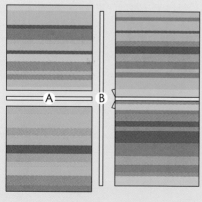

Block assembly

PIECED

Bar None

Diane Harris • quiltmaker.com

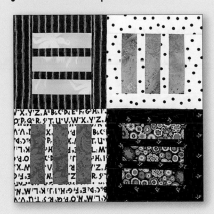

MATERIALS

2 white-on-black prints
  2 rectangles, 1½" x 4½", from *each* fabric (A)
  2 rectangles, 1" x 4½", from *each* fabric (B)
  2 rectangles, 1½" x 6½", from *each* fabric (C)

4 assorted blue prints
  3 rectangles, 1½" x 4½", from *each* fabric (A)

2 black-on-white prints
  2 rectangles, 1½" x 4½", from *each* fabric (A)
  2 rectangles, 1" x 4½", from *each* fabric (B)
  2 rectangles, 1½" x 6½", from *each* fabric (C)

INSTRUCTIONS

1. Join the pieces as shown to make a unit. Make four units.

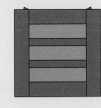

Make 4.

2. Join the units as shown to complete the block.

Block assembly

Birthday Girl

Bonnie Hunter • quiltville.com

MATERIALS

⬦ = *Cut in half diagonally.*

Assorted yellow prints
  16 squares, 2½" x 2½" (A)
  2 squares, 2⅞" x 2⅞" ⬦ (C)

Assorted purple prints
  8 rectangles, 2½" x 4½" (B)
  2 squares, 4⅞" x 4⅞" ⬦ (D)

Assorted red prints
  4 squares, 2⅞" x 2⅞" ⬦ (C)

Assorted cream prints
  6 squares, 2⅞" x 2⅞" ⬦ (C)

INSTRUCTIONS

1. Refer to "Stitch and Flip" on page 124. Use the yellow A squares and the purple B rectangles to make four each of units 1 and 2 as shown.

Unit 1.
Make 4.

Unit 2.
Make 4.

2. Pair the yellow and red C triangles to make four of unit 3.

Unit 3.
Make 4.

3. Pair the cream and remaining red C triangles together to make a pinwheel.

Pinwheel.
Make 1.

4. Join C and D pieces to each unit 3; then sew the units and pinwheel together as shown to complete the block.

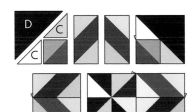

Block assembly

35

Blazing Star

Deanne Eisenman • snugglesquilts.com

MATERIALS

Black print
12 squares, 2⅜" x 2⅜" (A)
4 squares, 2" x 2" (C)

Beige-with-green print
3 squares, 4¼" x 4¼" (B)

Beige-with-red print
2 squares, 2⅜" x 2⅜" (A)
2 squares, 4¼" x 4¼" (B)
4 squares, 2" x 2" (C)
4 rectangles, 2" x 3½" (D)

Green print
6 squares, 2⅜" x 2⅜" (A)

Red print
4 squares, 2⅜" x 2⅜" (A)
1 square, 3½" x 3½" (E)

INSTRUCTIONS

1. Refer to "Fast Flying Geese" on page 124. Use the black A and beige-with-green B pieces to make 12 of unit 1. Use the green A and beige-with-red B pieces to make four of unit 2. Use the red A and beige-with-red B pieces to make four of unit 3.

2. Refer to "Triangle Squares" on page 124 and use the green A and beige-with-red B pieces to make four of unit 4.

Unit 1.
Make 12.

Unit 2.
Make 4.

Unit 3.
Make 4.

Unit 4.
Make 4.

3. Sew pieces C–E together with units 1–4 as shown to complete the block.

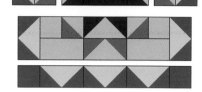

Block assembly

Boxed In

Julie Herman • jaybirdquilts.com

MATERIALS

Assorted prints
20 squares, 2½" x 2½" (A)

Tan tone-on-tone fabric
2 rectangles, 1½" x 4½" (B)
2 rectangles, 1½" x 6½" (C)
2 rectangles, 1½" x 10½" (D)
2 rectangles, 1½" x 12½" (E)

INSTRUCTIONS

Join the pieces as shown to complete the block.

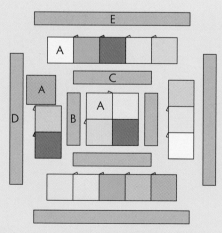

Block assembly

Butterfly Cabin

Jackie Robinson • animasquilts.com

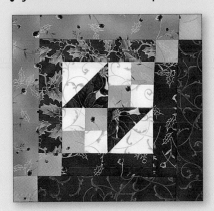

MATERIALS

◻ = *Cut in half diagonally.*

Cream print
  1 square, 3⅞" x 3⅞" ◻ (A)
  4 squares, 2" x 2" (B)

Red print
  1 square, 3⅞" x 3⅞" ◻ (A)
Gold print
  8 squares, 2" x 2" (B)
Medium-green print #1 and dark-green print #1
  1 rectangle, 2" x 6½", from *each* fabric (C)
  1 rectangle, 2" x 8", from *each* fabric (D)
Medium-green print #2 and dark-green print #2
  1 rectangle, 2" x 9½", from *each* fabric (E)
  1 rectangle, 2" x 11", from *each* fabric (F)

INSTRUCTIONS

Join the pieces as shown to complete the block.

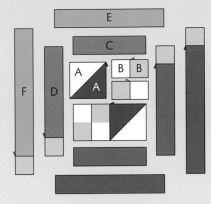

Block assembly

Candlestick

Karen Griska • onlinequiltmuseum.com

MATERIALS

Cream print #1
  1 square, 3⅞" x 3⅞" (A)
  4 squares, 2" x 2" (B)
  2 squares, 3½" x 3½" (C)
Cream print #2
  2 squares, 3⅞" x 3⅞" (A)
Cream print #3
  4 squares, 3½" x 3½" (C)
Cream print #4
  2 squares, 3½" x 3½" (C)

Dark-brown print
  1 square, 3⅞" x 3⅞" (A)
  4 squares, 2" x 2" (B)
Medium-brown print
  2 squares, 3⅞" x 3⅞" (A)

INSTRUCTIONS

1. Refer to "Triangle Squares" on page 124. Pair cream #1 and dark-brown A squares to make two of unit 1. Pair the remaining cream A squares with the medium-brown A squares to make four of unit 2.

Unit 1.
Make 2.

Unit 2.
Make 4.

2. Sew the cream and dark-brown B squares together to make two four-patch units as shown above right.

Four-patch unit.
Make 2.

3. Sew the units and C squares together as shown to complete the block.

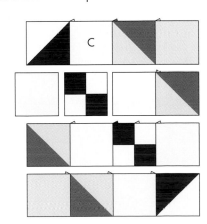

Block assembly

37

Carousel

Gerri Robinson • plantedseeddesigns.com

MATERIALS

White solid
  18 squares, 1⅞" x 1⅞" (A)
Assorted prints
  9 *sets of 2* matching squares,
    1⅞" x 1⅞" (9 sets of A)
  8 rectangles, 1½" x 2½" (B)
  8 rectangles, 1½" x 6½" (C)
Red print
  2 rectangles, 1½" x 10½" (D)
  2 rectangles, 1½" x 12½" (E)

INSTRUCTIONS

1. Refer to "Triangle Squares" on page 124. Pair two white with two matching print A squares to make four triangle-square units. Repeat to make nine sets of four matching units.

Make 9 sets of
4 matching units.

2. Sew together four matching units to make a pinwheel.

Pinwheel.
Make 9.

3. Join the pinwheels and pieces B–E as shown to complete the block.

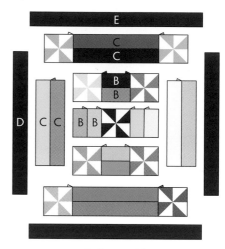

Block assembly

Chain Link

Emily Herrick • crazyoldladies.blogspot.com

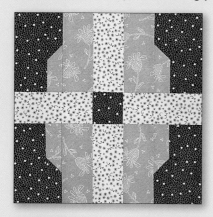

MATERIALS

Black print
  4 rectangles, 1½" x 3½" (A)
  4 rectangles, 2½" x 5½" (B)
  1 square, 2½" x 2½" (C)
Green print
  4 rectangles, 1½" x 3½" (A)
  4 rectangles, 2½" x 5½" (B)
Cream print
  4 rectangles, 2½" x 5½" (B)

INSTRUCTIONS

1. Referring to "Stitch and Flip" on page 124, use the black and green A rectangles to make two each of units 1 and 2.

Unit 1.
Make 2.

Unit 2.
Make 2.

2. Sew the units together with the B and C pieces as shown to complete the block.

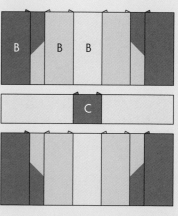

Block assembly

Chameleon

Deborah C. Vollbracht • creativefolkquilting.blogspot.com

MATERIALS

Pattern is on the enclosed disk.

Red-and-tan striped fabric
2 *each* of A and A reversed
Brown floral
4 *each* of A and A reversed
Black print
2 *each* of A and A reversed

INSTRUCTIONS

1. Join the black A reversed pieces to the brown-floral A reversed pieces to make rectangles. Join the brown-floral A pieces to the striped A pieces to make rectangles.

2. Join the pieced rectangles as shown to complete the block.

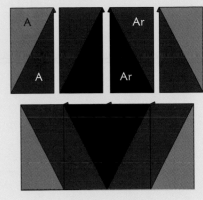

Block assembly

Chunky Monkey

Carrie Nelson • missrosiesquiltco.com

MATERIALS

Cream dotted fabric
8 squares, 2⅜" x 2⅜" (A)
16 rectangles, 1¼" x 3" (B)
4 assorted prints for block triangles
2 squares, 2⅜" x 2⅜", from *each* fabric (A)
4 assorted prints for block rails
4 rectangles, 1¼" x 3", from *each* fabric (B)

4 assorted prints for block centers
1 square, 3" x 3", from *each* fabric (C)
Blue print
4 rectangles, 1½" x 6" (D)
Red print
1 square, 1½" x 1½" (E)

INSTRUCTIONS

1. Referring to "Triangle Squares" on page 124, pair the cream A squares with the print A squares to make 16 units.

Make 16.

2. Referring to the diagram, join the units with the B and C pieces as shown, above right, to make four sections. Each section will measure 6" x 6".

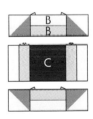

Make 4.

3. Join the sections with the D and E pieces as shown to complete the block.

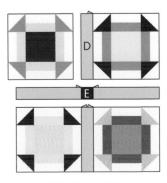

Block assembly

39

Colorful Star Tricks

Barbara Cline • delightfulpiecing.com

MATERIALS

Pattern A is on the enclosed disk.

◻ = *Cut in half diagonally.*
⊠ = *Cut into quarters diagonally.*

Light tone-on-tone fabrics in pink, teal, green, and yellow
  4 of A from *each* fabric

Medium tone-on-tone fabrics in pink, teal, green, and yellow
  6 of A from *each* fabric

Medium-brown and dark-brown tone-on-tone fabrics
  4 squares, 3¼" x 3¼", from *each* fabric ⊠ (B)

Cream print
  6 squares, 3¼" x 3¼" ⊠ (B)
  2 squares, 4⅜" x 4⅜" ◻ (C)

INSTRUCTIONS

1. Referring to "Set-in Seams" on page 124 and paying close attention to color placement, use the light- and medium-value A diamonds of the same color and brown B triangles to make unit 1. Join light- and medium-value A diamonds with cream B triangles to make unit 2. Make eight of each.

Unit 1.
Make 8.

Unit 2.
Make 8.

2. Join the units and the C triangles as shown to complete the block.

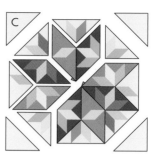

Block assembly

A Country Mile

Evonne M. Cook • clotheslinequilts.com

MATERIALS

Cream print
  4 squares, 2" x 2" (A)
  4 rectangles, 2" x 3½" (B)
  8 rectangles, 1½" x 5" (C)

Gold print
  12 squares, 2" x 2" (A)

Tan print
  8 squares, 2" x 2" (A)

Red print
  4 squares, 2" x 2" (A)

Black print
  4 rectangles, 1½" x 5" (C)

Dark-gray print
  9 squares, 1½" x 1½" (D)

INSTRUCTIONS

1. Join pieces A–D as shown to make a unit. Repeat to make four identical units.

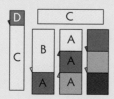

Make 4.

2. Join the units with the remaining C and D pieces as shown to complete the block.

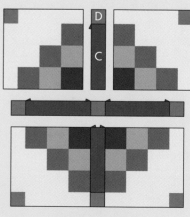

Block assembly

Courtyard Square

Pam Vieira-McGinnis • pamkittymorning.blogspot.com

MATERIALS

Red print
  1 square, 5¼" x 5¼ " (A)
Cream solid
  4 squares, 2⅞" x 2⅞" (B)
  4 rectangles, 2½" x 4½" (D)
  4 squares, 2½" x 2½" (F)
Cream print
  1 square, 4½" x 4½" (C)

Pink-striped fabric
  2 rectangles, 2½" x 4½" (D)
  2 rectangles, 2½" x 8½" (E)

INSTRUCTIONS

1. Referring to "Fast Flying Geese" on page 124, use the red A and cream B squares to make four flying-geese units.

Make 4.

2. Sew the units together with pieces C–F as shown to complete the block.

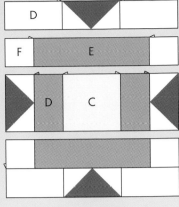

Block assembly

Criss Crossroads

Carol Newby • quiltersnewsletter.com

MATERIALS

Green tone-on-tone fabric
  24 squares, 1½" x 1½" (A)
Blue tone-on-tone fabric
  24 squares, 1½" x 1½" (A)
White print
  32 squares, 1½" x 1½" (A)
  16 squares, 1⅞" x 1⅞" (B)

Light-orange tone-on-tone fabric
  16 squares, 1½" x 1½" (A)
  8 squares, 1⅞" x 1⅞" (B)
Dark-orange tone-on-tone fabric
  16 squares, 1½" x 1½" (A)
  8 squares, 1⅞" x 1⅞" (B)

INSTRUCTIONS

1. Referring to "Triangle Squares" on page 124, pair the white and dark-orange B squares to make 16 of unit 1. Pair the white and light-orange B squares to make 16 of unit 2.

Unit 1.   Unit 2.
Make 16.   Make 16.

2. Join the squares and units as shown to make four sections. Sew the sections together to complete the block.

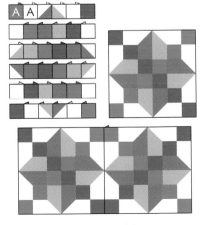

Block assembly

41

Daughter's Delight

Caroline Reardon and Maria Reardon Capp

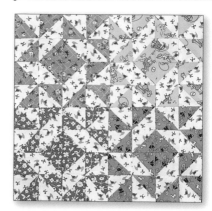

MATERIALS

White print
32 squares, 2⅜" x 2⅜"

Purple, green, pink, and blue prints
8 squares, 2⅜" x 2⅜", from *each* fabric

INSTRUCTIONS

1. Referring to "Triangle Squares" on page 124, pair the white and colored squares to make 64 units.

Make 64.

2. Join the units as shown to make four sections. Sew the sections together to complete the block.

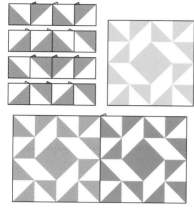

Block assembly

PIECED

Delicato

Susan Knapp & Mary Jane Mattingly • quiltbranch.com

MATERIALS

Green tone-on-tone fabric
4 squares, 3⅞" x 3⅞" (A)

Pink print #1
8 squares, 2" x 2" (B)
4 squares, 2¾" x 2¾" (D)

Gold tone-on-tone fabric
4 squares, 3⅞" x 3⅞" (A)
4 squares, 3½" x 3½" (C)

Pink print #2
4 squares, 3½" x 3½" (C)

Pink-striped fabric
4 squares, 2¾" x 2¾" (D)

INSTRUCTIONS

1. Referring to "Triangle Squares" on page 124, pair the green and gold A squares to make eight triangle squares. Use the "Stitch and Flip" technique (page 124) to sew a pink B square on the green corner of each triangle square as shown to complete eight of unit 1.

Unit 1.
Make 8.

2. Referring to the diagram and using the "Stitch and Flip" technique, make four of unit 2, sewing the pink #1 and pink-striped D squares on opposite corners of each gold C square as shown.

Keep the stripe oriented the same way on each one.

Unit 2.
Make 4.

3. Noting the orientation, join the units and the C squares as shown to complete the block.

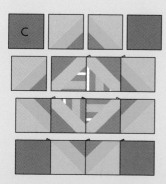

Block assembly

42

Diamond Blade

Leslee Price • ppnq.com

MATERIALS

White tone-on-tone fabric
6 squares, 2⅞" x 2⅞" (A)
12 squares, 2½" x 2½" (B)
24 squares, 1½" x 1½" (C)
Blue print
6 squares, 2⅞" x 2⅞" (A)
Pink print
24 squares, 1½" x 1½" (C)

INSTRUCTIONS

1. Referring to "Triangle Squares" on page 124, pair the white and blue A squares to make 12 of unit 1.

Unit 1.
Make 12.

2. Join the pink and white C squares as shown to make 12 of unit 2.

Unit 2.
Make 12.

3. Join units 1 and 2 with the B squares to make four sections as shown. Sew the sections together to complete the block.

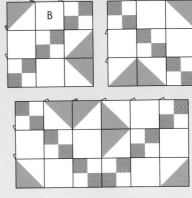

Block assembly

Double Star

Kim Brackett • magnoliabayquilts.blogspot.com

MATERIALS

Cream print
4 rectangles, 2½" x 6½" (A)
8 squares, 2½" x 2½" (B)
Red tone-on-tone fabric
6 squares, 2½" x 2½" (B)
Green tone-on-tone fabric
4 rectangles, 2½" x 6½" (A)
Green-striped fabric
4 rectangles, 2½" x 4½" (C)
Light-green print
2 squares, 2½" x 2½" (B)

INSTRUCTIONS

1. Using the "Stitch and Flip" technique on page 124 and referring to the diagrams, make four each of units 1–3.

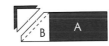

Unit 1.
Make 4.

Unit 2.
Make 4.

Unit 3.
Make 4.

2. Join a B square to the end of unit 3, then join units 1, 2, and 3 to make one block section as shown. Repeat to make four sections and sew them together to complete the block.

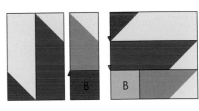

Block assembly

43

Dragonfly
Cindy Simms • cindysimms.net

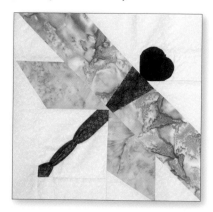

MATERIALS

Patterns are on the enclosed disk.

$\square$ = *Cut in half diagonally.*

Cream print
1 square, 5⅜" x 5⅜" $\square$ (A)
2 rectangles, 2¼" x 2¾" (E)
1 square, 2¾" x 2¾" (F)
1 square, 4½" x 4½" $\square$ (G)
1 rectangle, 2" x 5" (H)
1 rectangle, 2" x 6½" (I)
1 *each* of patterns M and M reversed
1 square, 3¾" x 3¾" $\square$ (N)

Assorted black prints
1 rectangle, 2½" x 7¼" (B)
1 square, 2¼" x 2¼" (C)
2 rectangles, 2½" x 4¼", for eyes (D)
1 of pattern J
Green batik
1 *each* of patterns K and K reversed
Blue batik
1 *each* of patterns L and L reversed

INSTRUCTIONS

1. Referring to the diagram, machine baste across B as shown. With wrong sides together, fold B in half lengthwise. Matching raw edges, layer B between the two A triangles as shown. Sew through all the layers to create the unit. From the back, pull on the basting threads to gather the tail into sections as shown. Knot the basting threads to secure. Press the seam open.

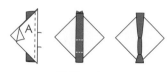

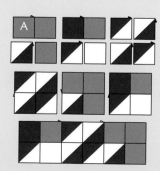

Tail basting

2. Referring to the diagram, fold each D rectangle in half lengthwise, wrong sides together. Baste through both layers as shown. Pull the basting threads to gather the edges, making two eyes.

Eye basting

3. Sandwich the eyes into the seams on adjoining sides of the C square as shown, making sure the raw edges are well within the seam allowance. Join the pieces to complete the block as shown.

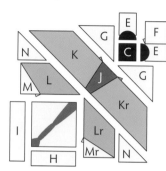

Block assembly

Easy 3-D
Maria Umhey

MATERIALS

Assorted light prints
3 squares, 2½" x 2½" (A)
9 squares, 2⅞" x 2⅞" (B)
Assorted dark-blue prints
3 squares, 2½" x 2½" (A)
9 squares, 2⅞" x 2⅞" (B)
Assorted medium-blue prints
12 squares, 2½" x 2½" (A)

INSTRUCTIONS

1. Referring to "Triangle Squares" on page 124, randomly join light and dark B squares to make 18 units.

Make 18.

2. Noting value placement, join the triangle squares and A squares to make the block.

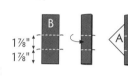

Block assembly

An interesting 3-D effect is created when 16 blocks are sewn together, as shown below.

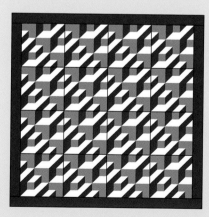

Suggested layout

Flutter

Patty Young • modkidboutique.com

MATERIALS

Large-scale aqua print
1 square, 7¾" x 7¾" (A)*

Red print
2 rectangles, 2¼" x 7¾" (B)
2 rectangles, 2¼" x 11½" (C)

Dark-teal print
4 rectangles, 2¼" x 7¾" (B)

Red-and-aqua print
4 rectangles, 2⅜" x 4" (D)

Patty personalized her block by adding a selvage strip to one side of A.

INSTRUCTIONS

1. Mark the center of each piece by folding it in half and pressing lightly. Matching centers, sew each D rectangle to a dark-teal B rectangle.

2. Referring to the piecing diagram, join the pieces as shown, matching their centers.

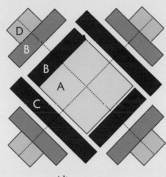

Align centers.

3. Centering the A square, trim the block to 12½" x 12½".

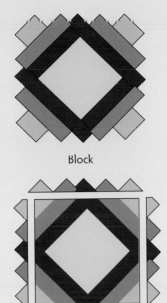

Block

Trim to 12½" x 12½".

Focal Point

Doug Leko • antlerquiltdesign.com

MATERIALS

Cream batik
10 squares, 2⅞" x 2⅞" (A)
1 square, 4½" x 4½" (C)
4 squares, 2½" x 2½" (D)
8 rectangles, 1½" x 4½" (E)

Red batik
4 squares, 2⅞" x 2⅞" (A)
4 squares, 2½" x 2½" (D)

Black print
2 squares, 2⅞" x 2⅞" (A)
1 square, 5¼" x 5¼" (B)

INSTRUCTIONS

1. Referring to "Triangle Squares" on page 124, pair the cream and red A squares to make eight of unit 1. Pair the cream and black A squares to make four of unit 2.

Unit 1.
Make 8.

Unit 2.
Make 4.

2. Referring to "Fast Flying Geese" on page 124, use the black B and cream A squares to make four of unit 3. Referring to "Stitch and Flip" on page 124, use the cream C and red D squares to make one of unit 4.

Unit 3.
Make 4.

Unit 4.
Make 1.

3. Join the units and D and E pieces as shown to complete the block.

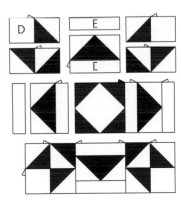

Block assembly

Follow Me Home

Elisa Wilson • backporchdesign.com

MATERIALS

Cream print
18 squares, 2⅜" x 2⅜" (A)
16 squares, 2" x 2" (B)
Dark-purple print
12 squares, 2⅜" x 2⅜" (A)

Green solid
6 squares, 2⅜" x 2⅜" (A)
Pink print
12 squares, 2" x 2" (B)

INSTRUCTIONS

1. Referring to "Triangle Squares" on page 124, use the cream and purple A squares to make 24 of unit 1. Use the cream and green A squares to make 12 of unit 2.

Unit 1.
Make 24.

Unit 2.
Make 12.

2. Sew the units and B squares together as shown to complete the block.

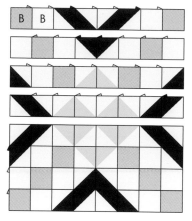

Block assembly

Four Corners

Celine Perkins • perkinsdrygoods.com

MATERIALS

Assorted green prints
6 squares, 2½" x 2½" (A)
2 squares, 2⅞" x 2⅞" (B)
Assorted beige prints
10 squares, 2½" x 2½" (A)
6 squares, 2⅞" x 2⅞" (B)
4 rectangles, 2½" x 4½" (C)

Assorted red prints
8 squares, 2½" x 2½" (A)
4 squares, 2⅞" x 2⅞" (B)
4 rectangles, 2½" x 4½" (C)

INSTRUCTIONS

1. Referring to "Triangle Squares" on page 124, pair each red and green B square with a beige B square to make four of unit 1 and eight of unit 2.

Unit 1.
Make 4.

Unit 2.
Make 8.

2. Referring to "Stitch and Flip" on page 124, use the red A squares and beige C rectangles to make four of unit 3 as shown above right. Use the beige A

squares and red C rectangles to make four of unit 4 as shown.

Unit 3.
Make 4.

Unit 4.
Make 4.

3. Sew the units and remaining A squares together as shown to complete the block.

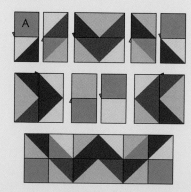

Block assembly

Four Patch Star

Lynn Schiefelbein • oakstreetquilts.com

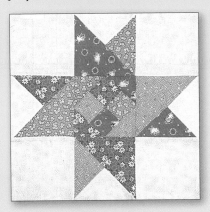

MATERIALS

◻ = Cut in half diagonally.
⊠ = Cut into quarters diagonally.

Pink, blue, yellow, and green prints
From *each* fabric, cut:*
    1 square, 2" x 2" (A)
    1 square, 2⅞" x 2⅞" ◻ (B)
    1 square, 5¼" x 5¼" ⊠ (C)
    1 square, 4⅞" x 4⅞" ◻ (D)

If you make just one block, you'll have extra B, C, and D pieces.

Cream tone-on-tone fabric
    1 square, 5¼" x 5¼" ⊠ (C)
    4 squares, 4½" x 4½" (E)

INSTRUCTIONS

1. Sew a print C triangle to the right of a cream C triangle along the short edges. Repeat to use one C triangle of each colored print. Sew a colored D triangle to each unit, paying close attention to the color placement in the block piecing diagram.

2. Join the A squares into a four-patch unit, and then add a B triangle to each side of the unit, again paying attention to color placement.

3. Join the pieced units and E squares as shown to complete the block.

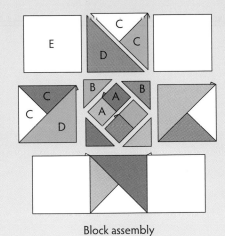

Block assembly

Fusion

Maria Hrabovsky • mariamichaelsdesigns.com

MATERIALS

Patterns are on the enclosed disk.

Dark-blue, red, green, and purple tone-on-tone fabrics
    1 *each* of patterns A, A reversed, C, and D from *each* fabric
Light-blue tone-on-tone fabric
    4 *each* of patterns B and B reversed

INSTRUCTIONS

1. Matching the black dots on A and A reversed to the black dots on C, join pieces A–D in the appropriate colors to make each section. You may find it helpful to mark the sewing lines and the points where the seams intersect; place a pin through the marks at each intersection. See "Set-In Seams (Y Seams)" on page 124 for more information.

2. Join the sections as shown to complete the block.

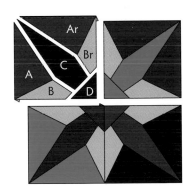

Block assembly

47

Garden Star

Pearl Louise Krush • thimblecottagevillage.com

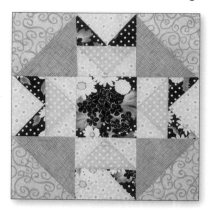

MATERIALS

Red print
    1 square, 4½" x 4½" (A)
    4 squares, 2⅞" x 2⅞" (C)
Pale-green dotted fabric
    1 square, 5¼" x 5¼" (B)
Pale-yellow print
    1 square, 5¼" x 5¼" (B)
    4 squares, 2⅞" x 2⅞" (C)

Blue tone-on-tone fabric
    2 squares, 4⅞" x 4⅞" (D)
Green tone-on-tone fabric
    2 squares, 4⅞" x 4⅞" (D)

INSTRUCTIONS

1. Referring to "Triangle Squares" on page 124, pair the blue and green D squares to make four of unit 1.

Unit 1.
Make 4.

2. Referring to "Fast Flying Geese" on page 124, use the green-dot B and yellow C pieces to make four of unit 2.

Use the yellow B and red C pieces to make four of unit 3.

Unit 2.   Unit 3.
Make 4.   Make 4.

3. Join the pieced units and A square as shown to complete the block.

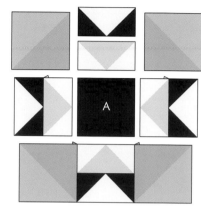

Block assembly

Geese 'Round the Rosie

Gudrun Erla • gequiltdesigns.com

MATERIALS

Burgundy print
    4 rectangles, 2½" x 4½" (A)
Cream tone-on-tone fabric
    16 squares, 2½" x 2½" (B)
    4 rectangles, 2½" x 8½" (F)
Green, rose, blue, and yellow prints
    1 rectangle, 2½" x 4½", from *each* fabric (A)
Floral print
    1 square, 3½" x 3½" (C)

Dark-green print
    2 rectangles, 1" x 3½" (D)
    2 rectangles, 1" x 4½" (E)

INSTRUCTIONS

1. Referring to "Stitch and Flip" on page 124, sew the cream B squares to the burgundy A rectangles to make four flying-geese units. Use the assorted print A rectangles and cream B squares to make four additional units.

Make 4 matching
and 4 assorted.

2. Join a burgundy unit and an assorted-print unit with an F rectangle as shown above right. Repeat to make four sections.

3. Sew pieces C–E together for the block center.

4. Sew one section to the right of the block center with a partial seam as shown. Sew the remaining sections to the top, left, and bottom of the block center. Then complete the partial seam to finish the block.

Make 4.

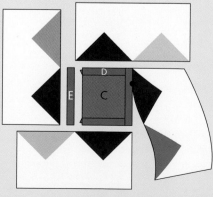

Block assembly
● = Partial seam

Halfsies

Theresa Eisinger

MATERIALS

Teal batik
4 squares, 2½" x 2½" (A)
Assorted medium-green batiks
4 squares, 2⅞" x 2⅞" (B)
Assorted cream batiks
4 squares, 2⅞" x 2⅞" (B)
Assorted peach batiks
4 squares, 2½" x 2½" (A)

Assorted light-green batiks
8 squares, 2⅞" x 2⅞" (B)
4 assorted orange batiks
2 squares, 2⅞" x 2⅞", from *each*
fabric (B)
Blue batik
4 squares, 2½" x 2½" (A)

INSTRUCTIONS

1. Referring to "Triangle Squares" on page 124, pair the medium-green B squares with the cream B squares to make eight triangle squares.

Make 8.

2. Pair the light-green B squares with the assorted orange B squares to make 16 triangle squares (four sets of four matching units).

3. Arrange the triangle squares and A squares as shown, with each matching set of four units forming a star. Join the pieces into rows. Sew the rows together to complete the block.

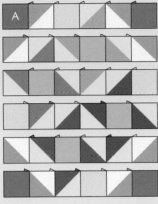

Block assembly

Heartfelt

Edyta Sitar • laundrybasketquilts.com

MATERIALS

◻ = *Cut in half diagonally.*
⊠ = *Cut into quarters diagonally.*

Tan batik
1 square, 5¼" x 5¼" (A)
6 squares, 2⅞" x 2⅞" ◻ (D)

Green batik
4 squares, 2⅞" x 2⅞" (B)
1 square, 5¼" x 5¼" ⊠ (C)
Medium-purple batik
1 square, 3⅜" x 3⅜" (E)
Purple floral batik
4 rectangles, 3⅜" x 6⅛" (F)

INSTRUCTIONS

1. Referring to "Fast Flying Geese" on page 124, use the tan A and green B squares to make four flying-geese units.

Make 4.

2. Join the flying-geese units and pieces C–F as shown to complete the block.

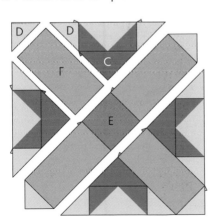

Block assembly

49

Homestead Album

Sarah Maxwell and Dolores Smith • homesteadhearth.com

MATERIALS

◻ = *Cut in half diagonally.*
⊠ = *Cut into quarters diagonally.*

Cream print
2 squares, 2⅜" x 2⅜" (A)
4 rectangles, 2" x 6½" (C)
1 square, 4¼" x 4¼" ⊠ (D)

Medium-blue print
2 squares, 2⅜" x 2⅜" (A)

Brown print and rust print #1
2 squares, 2⅜" x 2⅜", from *each* fabric (A)
4 rectangles, 1¼" x 3½", from *each* fabric (B)

Dark-blue print
4 rectangles, 2" x 6½" (C)

Rust print #2
1 square, 4¼" x 4¼" ⊠ (D)

Green print
2 squares, 3⅞" x 3⅞" ◻ (E)

INSTRUCTIONS

1. Referring to "Triangle Squares" on page 124, pair the cream and medium-blue A squares to make four of unit 1. Pair the brown and rust A squares to make four of unit 2.

Unit 1. Unit 2.
Make 4. Make 4.

2. Join units 1 and 2 with pieces B–E as shown to complete the block.

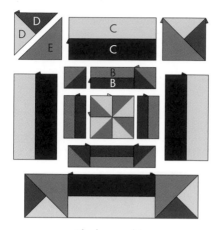

Block assembly

Infinity

Vickie Eapen • spunsugarquilt.com

MATERIALS

Cream large-scale print
4 squares, 2" x 2" (A)
4 squares, 3½" x 3½" (C)
1 square, 3⅞" x 3⅞" (E)

Red print
4 squares, 2" x 2" (A)
1 square, 3⅞" x 3⅞" (E)

Brown tone-on-tone fabric
4 squares, 2" x 2" (A)
2 rectangles, 2" x 3½" (B)
2 squares, 3½" x 3½" (C)
2 rectangles, 3½" x 6½" (D)

INSTRUCTIONS

1. Referring to "Triangle Squares" on page 124, use the cream and red E squares to make two triangle squares.

Make 2.

2. Join the triangle squares with pieces A–D as shown to complete the block.

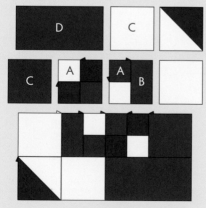

Block assembly

Jessie's Flag

Tina Curran and Jessica Lane • tinacurran.com

MATERIALS

◻ = *Cut in half diagonally.*

Assorted cream prints
14 squares, 2⅞" x 2⅞" ◻ (A)
(You'll have 1 extra triangle.)

Assorted red prints
14 squares, 2⅞" x 2⅞" ◻ (A)
(You'll have 1 extra triangle.)

Dark-blue print
5 squares, 2½" x 2½" (B)

Medium-blue print
4 squares, 2½" x 2½" (B)

INSTRUCTIONS

1. Join a cream A triangle to a red A triangle to make a triangle square. Repeat to make 27.

Make 27.

2. Join the blue B squares and the triangle squares into rows as shown. Sew the rows together to complete the block.

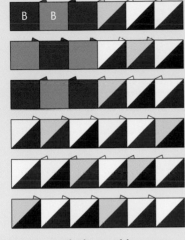

Block assembly

Jewel in the Pond

Wendy Slotboom

MATERIALS

Dark-pink print
2 squares, 6½" x 6½" (A)

2 brown dotted prints
2 squares, 3½" x 3½", from *each* fabric (B)

2 cream-and-pink prints
1 square, 6½" x 6½", from *each* fabric (A)

Green print
1 circle, 5½" diameter, for yo-yo

Rickrack: 4 pieces, 5" long, of pink
Button: ⅞" diameter

INSTRUCTIONS

1. Fold a B square in half diagonally and pin it to a corner of an A square, matching raw edges. Tuck a strip of the rickrack under the B fold and pin in place. Stitch close to the B folded edge through all layers as shown. Repeat to make a total of four of these sections.

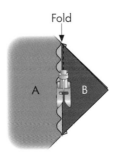

Fold

2. Join the units from step 1 as shown.

3. Referring to "Yo-Yos" on page 125, make a yo-yo from the 5½" green circle. Sew the yo-yo to the center of the block. Sew the button to the center of the yo-yo.

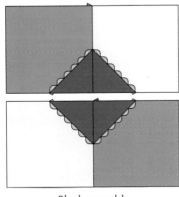

Block assembly

Joyful Noise

Margaret Miller • millerquilts.com

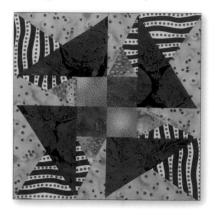

MATERIALS

Patterns are on the enclosed disk.

▢ *= Cut in half diagonally. If you stack your fabrics before cutting, have all of the right sides facing up.*

Red print
2 rectangles, 4¾" x 7" ▢ (A)
(see diagram at right)

Red-and-cream striped fabric
4 *each* of patterns B and F

Gold print
4 of pattern C
2 rectangles, 2⅝" x 5⅜" ▢ (D)
(see diagram below)

Medium-green tone-on-tone fabric #1
4 of pattern E

Medium-green tone-on-tone fabric #2 and dark-green tone-on-tone fabric
2 squares, 2½" x 2½", from *each* fabric (G)

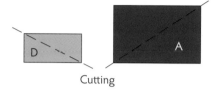

Cutting

INSTRUCTIONS

1. Sew pieces A–C together as shown above right to make four of unit 1. Sew pieces D–F together as shown to make four of unit 2.

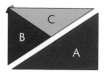

Unit 1.
Make 4.

Unit 2.
Make 4.

2. Join units 1 and 2 with the G squares as shown to complete the block.

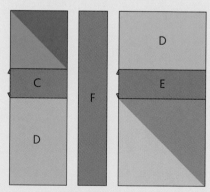

Block assembly

Jungle Boogie

June Dudley • quiltmaker.com

MATERIALS

Medium-blue print
1 square, 4⅞" x 4⅞" (A)

Dark-blue print
1 square, 4⅞" x 4⅞ (A)

Light-green print
1 square, 6⅞" x 6⅞" (B)

Medium-green print
1 square, 6⅞" x 6⅞" (B)

Rust-striped fabric
1 rectangle, 2½" x 4½" (C)
1 rectangle, 2½" x 6½" (E)
1 rectangle, 2½" x 12½" (F)

Multicolored print
1 rectangle, 4½" x 6½" (D)

Blue batik
1 rectangle, 4½" x 6½" (D)

INSTRUCTIONS

1. Referring to "Triangle Squares" on page 124, use the medium-blue and dark-blue A squares to make unit 1. Use the light-green and medium-green B squares to make unit 2. (You'll have one unit left over of each—make another block!)

2. Sew the units and pieces C–F together as shown to complete the block.

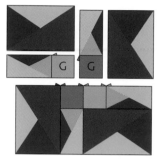

Block assembly

Unit 1.
Make 1.

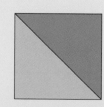

Unit 2.
Make 1.

Kraut Cutter

Mickey Charleston

MATERIALS

Pattern is on the enclosed disk.

Assorted pink, orange, and brown prints and tone-on-tone fabrics
  4 assorted squares, 6½" x 6½" (A)
  12 assorted strips, 1½" x 4½" (B)

INSTRUCTIONS

1. Join two A squares and trim at an angle to make a section as shown. Repeat for the remaining A squares.

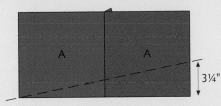

Make 2.

2. Make a template for B and use it to trim each 1½" x 4½" strip to size. Join the B pieces as shown.

3. Join the A and B sections to complete the block.

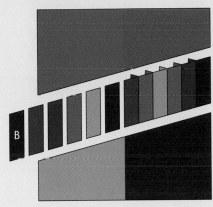

Block assembly

Late Bloomer

Pam Buda • heartspunquilts.com

MATERIALS

◻ = *Cut in half diagonally.*

Tan print
  8 rectangles, 2" x 4½" (A)
  4 squares, 2½" x 2½" (C)

Blue print
  4 rectangles, 1½" x 4½" (B)
  2 squares, 4⅞" x 4⅞" ◻ (E)
  4 rectangles, 1½" x 2" (G)
Red print
  8 squares, 2½" x 2½" (C)
  4 squares, 2" x 2" (F)
  1 square, 1½" x 1½" (H)
Green print
  4 squares, 2⅞" x 2⅞" ◻ (D)

INSTRUCTIONS

1. Sew an A rectangle to each side of a B rectangle as shown. Referring to "Stitch and Flip" on page 124, add a red C square to two adjacent corners to make a unit as shown. Make four.

Make 4.

2. Join the units with pieces C–H as shown to complete the block.

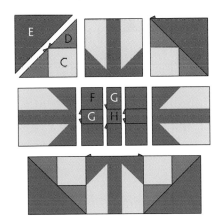

Block assembly

53

Little Boxes

Brenda Groelz • handiquilter.com

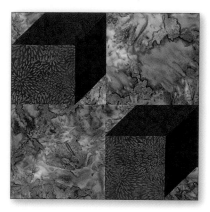

MATERIALS

Choose a light (pink), medium (red), and dark (black) fabric for the boxes to create the illusion of depth.

Gray batik
  2 squares, 2⅞" x 2⅞" (A)
  2 squares, 6½" x 6½" (D)

Red batik
  2 squares, 2⅞" x 2⅞" (A)
  2 squares, 2½" x 2½" (B)
Black batik
  2 squares, 2⅞" x 2⅞" (A)
  2 squares, 2½" x 2½" (B)
Pink batik
  2 squares, 4½" x 4½" (C)

INSTRUCTIONS

1. Referring to "Triangle Squares" on page 124, pair a gray and a red A square to make two of unit 1. Pair a red and a black A square to make two of unit 2. Pair a black and a gray A square to make two of unit 3.

Unit 1.   Unit 2.   Unit 3.
Make 2.   Make 2.   Make 3.

2. Join the units and pieces B–D as shown to complete the block.

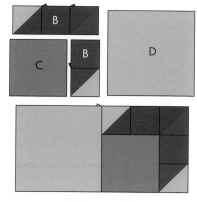

Block assembly

May Flowers

Carolyn Beam • quiltmaker.com

MATERIALS

White tone-on-tone fabric
  4 rectangles, 2½" x 5½" (A)
  12 squares, 1½" x 1½" (C)
Green print
  4 squares, 2½" x 2½" (B)
2 pink prints
  4 rectangles, 2½" x 5½", from *each* fabric (A)
  4 rectangles, 1½" x 2½", from *each* fabric (D)

Red tone-on-tone fabric
  4 squares, 1½" x 1½" (C)
Green tone-on-tone fabric
  4 squares, 1½" x 1½" (C)
  1 square, 2½" x 2½" (B)

INSTRUCTIONS

1. Referring to "Stitch and Flip" on page 124, use the white A and green-print B pieces to make four of unit 1. Add a white C square to the top corners of two of each of the pink-print A pieces to make four of unit 2. Add a white C to the bottom-left corner and a green C to the bottom-right corner of the remaining pink A pieces to make four of unit 3.

2. Join a red C and two D pieces with a matching unit 2 and unit 3. Add a unit 1 to make a section; make four sections. Noting the orientation, sew one section to the right side of B with a partial seam as shown. Sew the remaining sections to the bottom, left, and top of B. Complete the partial seam to finish the block.

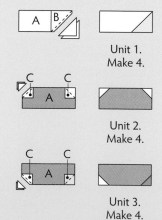

Unit 1.
Make 4.

Unit 2.
Make 4.

Unit 3.
Make 4.

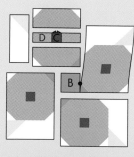

Block assembly
● = Partial seam

Merry-Go-Round

Eleanor Burns • quiltinaday.com

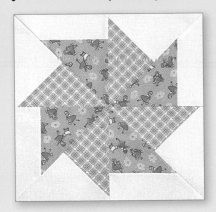

MATERIALS

◺ = *Cut in half diagonally.*
⊠ = *Cut into quarters diagonally.*

White tone-on-tone fabric
1 square, 7¼" x 7¼" ⊠ (A)
4 rectangles, 2" x 6⅞" (C) (see diagram below)

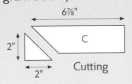

Cutting

Yellow print
1 square, 7¼" x 7¼" ⊠ (A)
Green print
2 squares, 5⅜" x 5⅜" ◺ (B)

INSTRUCTIONS

1. Join the white and yellow A triangles in pairs along their short edges, with the white triangles on the right.

2. Join a C piece to a short side of each B triangle.

3. Join the pieced triangles to make four units. Join the units as shown to complete the block.

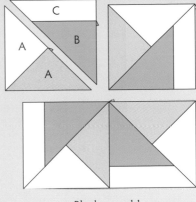

Block assembly

Mini Pod

Emily Cier • carolinapatchworks.com

MATERIALS

Pink-and-black print
8 squares, 1½" x 1½" (A)
6 rectangles, 1½" x 3½" (B)
2 rectangles, 1" x 1½" (C)

Cream solid
7 squares, 1½" x 1½" (A)
4 rectangles, 1" x 1½" (C)
2 rectangles, 1½" x 12½" (D)
Black print
1 rectangle, 1½" x 12½" (D)
1 rectangle, 6½" x 12½" (E)

INSTRUCTIONS

1. Sew the A squares together in sets of three, alternating print and cream squares. Make three sets with pink-and-black on the ends and two sets with cream on the ends. Join the C rectangles in the same manner, making two segments with cream squares on the ends.

2. Sew the units from step 1 together with the pink-and-black B pieces, alternating them as shown.

3. Join the pieced strip with the D and E pieces as shown to complete the block.

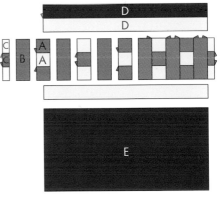

Block assembly

Moss Rose

Laura Stone Roberts • mccallsquilting.com

MATERIALS

10 assorted batiks, from light yellow and light pink to very dark pink
   1 strip, 1¼" x 32", from *each* fabric
Green batik
   4 rectangles, 2½" x 5½" (B)
Red batik
   8 squares, 1½" x 1½" (C)
Gold batik
   1 square, 2½" x 2½" (D)
Template plastic
   1 square, 5½" x 5½"

INSTRUCTIONS

1. Sew the strips together as shown with yellow at one end and the darkest pink at the other end to make a strip set. Position the template on the strip set and cut four A squares as shown.

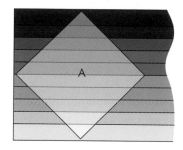

Cut 4.

2. Referring to "Stitch and Flip" on page 124, sew red C squares to adjacent corners at one end of each green B rectangle, as shown above right. Make four.

Make 4.

3. Sew the units together with the gold D square as shown to complete the block.

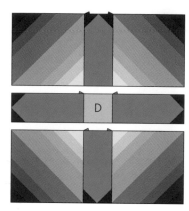

Block assembly

Mount Vernon Steps

Maria Umhey

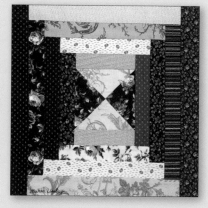

MATERIALS

⊠ = *Cut into quarters diagonally.*

Cream print
   1 square, 5¼" x 5¼" ⊠ (A)
      (You'll have 2 extra triangles.)

Dark-red floral
   1 square, 5¼" x 5¼" ⊠ (A)
      (You'll have 2 extra triangles.)

Assorted light prints
   2 rectangles, 1½" x 4½" (B)
   2 rectangles, 1½" x 6½" (C)
   2 rectangles, 1½" x 8½" (D)
   2 rectangles, 1½" x 10½" (E)

Assorted dark prints
   2 rectangles, 1½" x 6½" (C)
   2 rectangles, 1½" x 8½" (D)
   2 rectangles, 1½" x 10½" (E)
   2 rectangles, 1½" x 12½" (F)

INSTRUCTIONS

1. Join the A triangles to make the block center.

2. Add two light B rectangles followed by two dark C rectangles to the block center. Continue adding rectangles in this manner to complete the block.

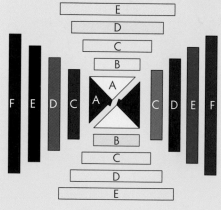

Block assembly

Navajo Nights

Eileen Fowler • quiltmaker.com

MATERIALS

Dark-blue batik
4 rectangles, 2½" x 6½" (A)
4 rectangles, 2½" x 4½" (B)
4 squares, 2½" x 2½" (E)

Medium-purple batik #1
2 rectangles, 2½" x 4½" (B)

Medium-purple batik #2
2 rectangles, 2½" x 8½" (C)

Gray batik
2 rectangles, 2½" x 12½" (D)

INSTRUCTIONS

1. Referring to "Stitch and Flip" on page 124 and the diagrams, make two each of units 1–3 as follows: Use the dark-blue A and medium-purple #1 B pieces for unit 1. Use the dark-blue B and medium-purple #2 C pieces for unit 2. Use the dark-blue E and gray D pieces for unit 3.

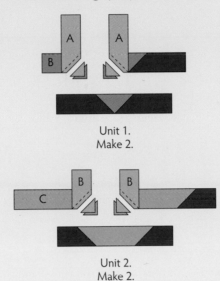

Unit 1.
Make 2.

Unit 2.
Make 2.

Unit 3.
Make 2.

2. Join the units as shown to complete the block.

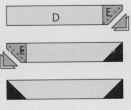

Block assembly

Night Owl

Marjorie Rhine • quiltdesignnw.com

MATERIALS

Appliqué patterns are on the enclosed disk.

◹ = *Cut in half diagonally.*

Tan tone-on-tone fabric
1 rectangle, 6½" x 9½" (A)
4 squares, 1¼" x 1¼" (B)
2 rectangles, 1¼" x 2" (C)

Gray print
2 rectangles, 1¼" x 2" (C)
1 of pattern G

Brown plaid
2 squares, 1¼" x 1¼" (B)
1 square, 2⅜" x 2⅜" ◹ (D)

Assorted dark prints
8 squares, 2⅜" x 2⅜" ◹ (D)

Black tone-on-tone fabric
2 rectangles, 1¼" x 2" (C)
3 squares, 2⅜" x 2⅜" ◹ (D)
2 rectangles, 2" x 10¼" (E)
1 rectangle, 2¾" x 12½" (F)

White tone-on-tone fabric
2 of pattern H

Gold tone-on-tone fabric
2 of pattern I

Black solid
2 of pattern J

Fusible web

INSTRUCTIONS

1. Referring to "Stitch and Flip" on page 124, use the gray C and tan B pieces to make two flying-geese units as shown. Add plaid B squares to the top corners of A.

Make 2.

2. Prepare pieces G–J for fusible appliqué. Fold A in half vertically and use the crease and the block assembly diagram to arrange the pieces on A. Fuse the pieces to A. Use matching thread and a zigzag stitch to sew around the appliqués.

3. Join A, the flying-geese units, and pieces C–F as shown to complete the block.

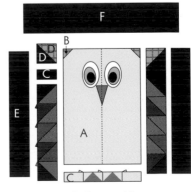

Block assembly

Northern Flair

Gudrun Erla • gequiltdesigns.com

MATERIALS

 = Cut in half diagonally.

 = Cut into quarters diagonally.

Rust tone-on-tone fabric
- 8 rectangles, 1½" x 2½" (A)
- 4 rectangles, 1½" x 3½" (C)

Cream tone-on-tone fabric
- 8 rectangles, 1½" x 2½" (A)
- 32 squares, 1½" x 1½" (B)
- 4 squares, 2⅞" x 2⅞" (D)

Green print
- 4 rectangles, 1½" x 2½" (A)
- 8 rectangles, 1½" x 3½" (C)

Gold print
- 8 squares, 1½" x 1½" (B)

Brown print
- 1 square, 7¼" x 7¼" (E)

Blue print
- 1 square, 2½" x 2½" (F)

INSTRUCTIONS

1. Referring to "Stitch and Flip" on page 124, use the rust and green A and C rectangles and the cream B squares to make units 1 through 7 as shown.

Unit 1.
Make 6.

Unit 2.
Make 4.

Unit 3.
Make 4.

Unit 4.
Make 4.

Unit 5.
Make 2.

Unit 6.
Make 2.

Unit 7.
Make 2.

2. Sew a cream D triangle to each unit 3 and trim as shown to make four of unit 8.

Sew a cream D triangle to each unit 4 and trim as shown to make four of unit 9.

Unit 8.
Make 4.

Unit 9.
Make 4.

3. Join the pieces and units as shown to complete the block.

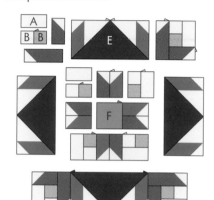

Block assembly

Nouveau Riche

Toby Lischko • gatewayquiltsnstuff.com

MATERIALS

Patterns are on the enclosed disk.

Assorted gold batiks
- 4 of pattern A
- 4 of pattern D

Assorted black batiks
- 2 of pattern B
- 2 of pattern C

INSTRUCTIONS

1. Join pieces A and B to make two units and pieces C and D to make two units. Find tips for curved piecing on page 123.

2. Join the four units as shown to complete the block.

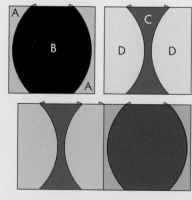

Block assembly

Suggested layout

PIECED

Odd Fellow's Chain

Karen Combs • karencombs.com

MATERIALS

◻ = Cut in half diagonally.
⊠ = Cut into quarters diagonally.

Lime batik
    4 squares, 2⅜" x 2⅜" (A)
    1 square, 4¼" x 4¼" (B)
    4 squares, 2" x 2" (C)
    4 squares, 2⅜" x 2⅜" ◻ (D)
Medium-green batik
    8 squares, 2⅜" x 2⅜" (A)

Dark-green batik
    4 squares, 2" x 2" (C)
    1 square, 4¼" x 4¼" ⊠ (E)
Medium-blue batik
    4 squares, 3⅞" x 3⅞" ◻ (F)
Dark-blue batik
    1 square, 4¼" x 4¼" (B)
    4 squares, 2" x 2" (C)
Purple batik
    4 squares, 2⅜" x 2⅜" (A)
Pink batik
    1 square, 3½" x 3½" (G)

INSTRUCTIONS

1. Referring to "Triangle Squares" on page 124, pair the lime and medium-green A squares to make eight of unit 1.

Unit 1.
Make 8.

2. Referring to "Fast Flying Geese" on page 124, use the medium-green A and lime B squares to make four of unit 2. Use the purple A and dark-blue B squares to make four of unit 3.

Unit 2.   Unit 3.
Make 4.   Make 4.

3. Join the pieces and units as shown to make the block.

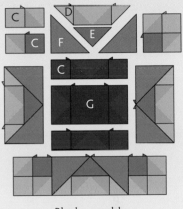

Block assembly

Old Glory

Maria Peagler • quiltsandcreativity.com

MATERIALS

◻ = Cut in half diagonally.
⊠ = Cut into quarters diagonally.

Cream print #1
    1 square, 3¼" x 3¼" ⊠ (A)
    2 squares, 2⅞" x 2⅞" ◻ (B)

Navy-striped fabric
    1 square, 3¼" x 3¼" ⊠ (A)
Navy print
    2 squares, 3¾" x 3¾" ◻ (C)
2 red prints
    1 rectangle, 2⅜" x 6¾", from each fabric (D)
    1 rectangle, 2⅛" x 12½", from each fabric (E)
Cream print #2
    1 rectangle, 2⅜" x 6¾" (D)
    2 rectangles, 2⅛" x 12½" (E)

INSTRUCTIONS

1. Join pieces A–C to make the pinwheel.

2. Join the D pieces to make a unit and sew it to the side of the pinwheel unit.

3. Join the E pieces and sew them to the bottom of the pinwheel unit to complete the block.

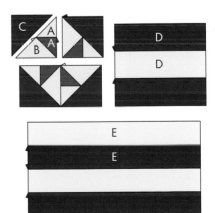

Block assembly

Payton's Star

Sharyn Craig • sharyncraig.com

MATERIALS

Blue batik
    1 square, 5¼" x 5¼" (A)
    4 squares, 2½" x 2½" (D)
Cream print
    1 square, 5¼" x 5¼" (A)
    4 squares, 2⅞" x 2⅞" (B)
    2 squares, 4⅞" x 4⅞" (C)
Light-green print
    4 squares, 2⅞" x 2⅞" (B)

Tan batik
    2 squares, 4⅞" x 4⅞" (C)
Green batik
    1 square, 4½" x 4½" (E)

INSTRUCTIONS

1. Referring to "Fast Flying Geese" on page 124, use the blue A and cream B squares to make four of unit 1. Use the cream A and green B squares to make four of unit 2.

Unit 1.
Make 4.

Unit 2.
Make 4.

2. Referring to "Triangle Squares" on page 124, use the cream and tan C squares to make four triangle squares. Referring to "Stitch and Flip" on page

124, sew a blue D square on the tan corner of each triangle square to make unit 3.

Unit 3.
Make 4.

3. Noting the orientation of the units, join them with piece E as shown to complete the block.

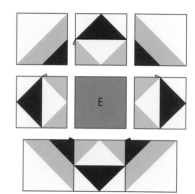

Pinwheel Splash

Joli Sayasane • quiltersnewsletter.com

MATERIALS

◻ = Cut in half diagonally.

Brown print
    4 rectangles, 1⅞" x 6⅞" (A)
Medium-blue tone-on-tone fabric
    4 rectangles, 1⅞" x 6⅞" (A)

Rust tone-on-tone fabric
    4 squares, 2⅞" x 2⅞" ◻ (B)
Light-blue tone-on-tone fabric
    4 squares, 2⅞" x 2⅞" ◻ (B)
Blue print
    4 squares, 4⅞" x 4⅞" ◻ (C)

INSTRUCTIONS

1. Cut each end of the A pieces as shown.

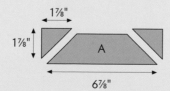

2. Join pieces A–C as shown to complete the block.

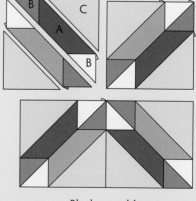

Block assembly

Porch Swing

Cyndi Walker • stitchstudios.com

MATERIALS

Yellow-checked fabric
2 squares, 2⅞" x 2⅞" (A)
4 rectangles, 2½" x 4½" (B)

Cream solid
4 squares, 2⅞" x 2⅞" (A)
4 rectangles, 2½" x 4½" (B)

Pink solid and red print
3 squares, 2⅞" x 2⅞", from *each* fabric (A)

Blue tone-on-tone and green print
4 squares, 2⅞" x 2⅞", from *each* fabric (A)

Blue plaid and blue print
4 squares, 2½" x 2½", from *each* fabric (C)

INSTRUCTIONS

1. Referring to "Triangle Squares" on page 124, pair the A squares in color combinations as shown to make units 1 through 5.

Unit 1.   Unit 2.   Unit 3.
Make 2.   Make 8.   Make 2.

Unit 4.   Unit 5.
Make 4.   Make 4.

2. Referring to "Stitch and Flip" on page 124 and noting the placement of each blue fabric, use the blue-plaid and blue-print C squares and the cream B rectangles to make four of unit 6.

Unit 6.
Make 4.

3. Join the units with the B rectangles as shown to complete the block.

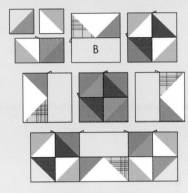

Block assembly

Posy Power

Beth Hayes • mccallsquilting.com

MATERIALS

Assorted floral prints
9 squares, 4½" x 4½" (A)*

Light-green solid
18 squares, 1¾" x 1¾" (B)

Dark-green solid
18 squares, 1¾" x 1¾" (B)

You may want to fussy cut your squares to make best use of the floral prints.

INSTRUCTIONS

1. Using the "Stitch and Flip" technique on page 124, add light-green B squares to the lower-right and upper-left corners of every A square. Trim and press open. In the same way, add dark-green B squares to the remaining corners of each A square to complete the units.

Make 9.

2. Arrange the units as shown, with a light-green square in the upper-left corner on each unit. Join the units to complete the block.

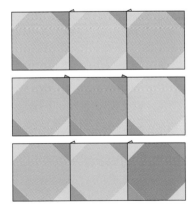

Block assembly

Potted Posies

Lynne Hagmeier • ktquilts.com

MATERIALS

◻ = Cut in half diagonally.

Tan print
- 2 squares, 3⅞" x 3⅞" ◻ (A)
- 4 squares, 3½" x 3½" (B)
- 4 rectangles, 3½" x 6½" (C)

4 dark-red prints
- 1 square, 3⅞" x 3⅞", from *each* fabric ◻ (A) (You'll have 4 extra triangles.)

4 dark-green prints
- 1 square, 3½" x 3½", from *each* fabric (B)

Dark-green plaid
- 4 rectangles, ⅜" x 4" (D)

4 gold prints
- 1 square, 1⅛" x 1⅛", from *each* fabric (E)

INSTRUCTIONS

1. Referring to "Triangle Squares" on page 124, pair each dark-red A triangle with a tan A triangle to make four of unit 1.

Unit 1.
Make 4.

2. For unit 2, sew a tan B square to each unit 1; then sew a tan C rectangle to the bottom of the unit. Position a D strip as shown and use matching thread to stitch down the center of D.

3. Referring to "Stitch and Flip" on page 124, add a dark-green B square as shown. Make four; each unit should measure 6½" square.

Unit 2.
Make 4.

4. Position an E square on each unit 2 and use matching thread to stitch ⅛" from the raw edges. Then join the units as shown to complete the block.

Block assembly

Red Rover

Monique Dillard • opengatequilts.com

MATERIALS

◻ = Cut in half diagonally.

Cream print
- 2 squares, 5⅜" x 5⅜" ◻ (A)
- 16 squares, 2⅜" x 2⅜" (B)

4 red prints
- 1 square, 5⅜" x 5⅜", from *each* fabric ◻ (A) (You'll have 4 extra triangles.)
- 4 squares, 2⅜" x 2⅜", from each fabric (B)

INSTRUCTIONS

1. Join each cream A triangle with a different red A triangle to make four of unit 1.

Unit 1.
Make 4.

2. Referring to "Triangle Squares" on page 124, use the cream and red B squares to make 32 of unit 2.

Unit 2.
Make 32.
(4 are extra).

3. Using just one red print in each of the block quadrants, join the units as shown to complete the block. (You'll have one leftover unit 2 from each red fabric.)

Block assembly

Ripples

Laura Stone Roberts • mccallsquilting.com

MATERIALS

Brown tone-on-tone fabric
- 14 squares, 1½" x 1½" (A)
- 14 rectangles, 1½" x 2½" (B)
- 4 rectangles, 1½" x 3½" (C)

Pink tone-on-tone fabric
- 16 squares, 1½" x 1½" (A)
- 10 rectangles, 1½" x 2½" (B)
- 8 rectangles, 1½" x 3½" (C)

Pale-blue tone-on-tone fabric
- 30 squares, 1½" x 1½" (A)

INSTRUCTIONS

1. Referring to the diagrams, sew the A, B, and C pieces together for each section as shown. The completed sections should measure 6½" x 6½".

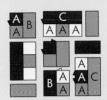
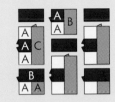

Section 1.
Make 2.

Section 2.
Make 1.

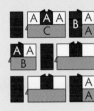

Section 3.
Make 1.

2. Orienting the sections as shown, join them to complete the block.

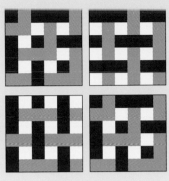

Block assembly

Rolling River

Joyce Robinson • joycerobinson.com

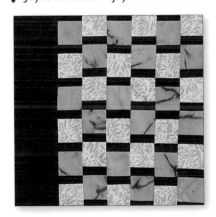

MATERIALS

Purple batik
- 6 strips, 1" x 13", for strip set
- 1 rectangle, 3½" x 12½" (A)

Light-gold tone-on-tone batik
- 3 strips, 2" x 13", for strip set

Gold batik
- 3 strips, 2" x 13", for strip set

INSTRUCTIONS

1. Sew the purple, light gold, and gold strips together as shown to make a strip set. Cut the strip set at 2" intervals to make six segments.

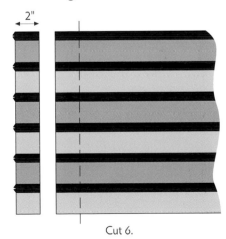

2"

Cut 6.

2. Join the segments, alternating their direction as shown. Sew piece A to the left side to complete the block.

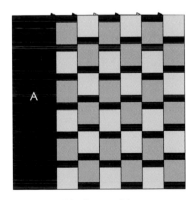

A

Block assembly

63

Rose Twirls

Elisa Wilson • backporchdesign.com

MATERIALS

Patterns are on the enclosed disk.

Dark-pink batik and white batik
4 squares, 6⅞" x 6⅞", from *each* fabric (A)

Blue batik
4 squares, 4½" x 4½" (D)

Light-pink batik and orange batik
4 squares, 1¾" x 1¾", from *each* fabric (E)

INSTRUCTIONS

1. Referring to "Triangle Squares" on page 124, pair the dark-pink and white A squares to make eight units. Make templates of B and C. Noting the color orientation of the units, cut four of B and four of C as shown.

Make 8.   Cut 4.   Cut 4.

2. Referring to "Curved Piecing" on page 123, sew each C to a B. Referring to the diagrams, align D on the corner of B/C, right sides together. Mark a line on the wrong side of D, starting 1" down one side to the opposite corner. Sew on the marked line. Trim the seam allowances to ¼". Flip D open and trim as shown.

Make 4.

3. Referring to "Stitch and Flip" on page 124, add light-pink and orange E squares to the corners as shown to complete four sections.

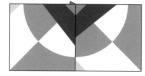

Make 4.

4. Join the sections as shown to complete the block.

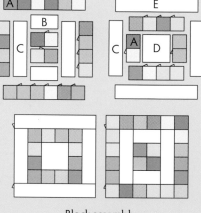

Block assembly

Roundabout

Carolyn Beam • quiltmaker.com

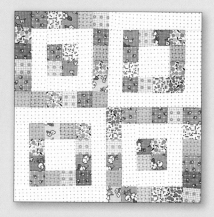

MATERIALS

Assorted prints
72 squares, 1½" x 1½" (A)

White dotted fabric
4 rectangles, 1½" x 2½" (B)
8 rectangles, 1½" x 4½" (C)
2 squares, 2½" x 2½" (D)
4 rectangles, 1½" x 6½" (E)

INSTRUCTIONS

1. Join pieces A–E as shown to make four sections.

2. Sew the sections together to complete the block.

Block assembly

PIECED

64

Scarlet Days

Kimberly Jolly • fatquartershop.com

MATERIALS

Red print

1 square, 2½" x 2½" (A)
6 squares, 1⅞" x 1⅞" (B)
2 squares, 5¼" x 5¼" (D)
6 squares, 2⅞" x 2⅞" (E)

Tan solid

4 squares, 2½" x 2½" (A)
2 squares, 1⅞" x 1⅞" (B)
1 square, 3¼" x 3¼" (C)
14 squares, 2⅞" x 2⅞" (E)

INSTRUCTIONS

1. Referring to "Fast Flying Geese" on page 124, use four red B squares and the tan C square to make four of flying-geese unit 1. Use the red D squares and eight tan E squares to make eight of flying-geese unit 2.

Flying-geese unit 1.
Make 4.

Flying-geese unit 2.
Make 8.

2. Referring to "Triangle Squares" on page 124, pair red and tan B squares to make four of unit 1. Pair red and tan E squares to make 12 of unit 2.

Unit 1.
Make 4.

Unit 2.
Make 12.

3. Sew the units and pieces together as shown to complete the block.

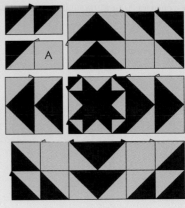

Block assembly

Sew-Easy Butterflies

Darlene Zimmerman • feedsacklady.com

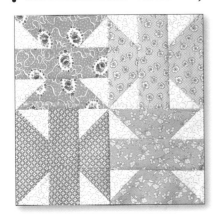

MATERIALS

Blue, yellow, pink, and green prints

3 rectangles, 2½" x 6½", from *each* fabric (A)

White print

16 squares, 2½" x 2½" (B)

INSTRUCTIONS

1. Referring to "Stitch and Flip" on page 124, sew the white B squares to the ends of two A rectangles of each color.

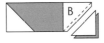

Make 8.

2. Sew the units and remaining A pieces together as shown to complete the block.

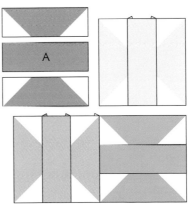

Block assembly

Shifting Star

Scott Murkin • patchworkpossibilities.com

MATERIALS

Rust print
4 rectangles, 3½" x 6½" (A)

Cream tone-on-tone fabric
4 squares, 3½" x 3½" (B)

Light-brown print #1
4 squares, 3½" x 3½" (B)

Light-brown print #2
4 rectangles, 2½" x 6½" (C)

Dark-brown striped fabric
4 rectangles, 1½" x 6½" (D)

INSTRUCTIONS

1. Referring to "Stitch and Flip" on page 124, use the A and B pieces as shown to make two each of units 1 and 2.

Unit 1.
Make 2.

Unit 2.
Make 2.

2. Join the units and C and D pieces as shown to make four sections. Join the sections to complete the block.

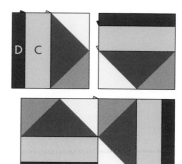

Block assembly

Snow Shoo

Theresa Eisinger • quiltmaker.com

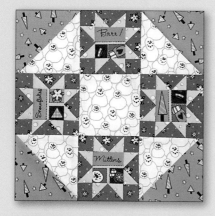

MATERIALS

Teal print
2 squares, 4⅞" x 4⅞" (A)

White print
2 squares, 4⅞" x 4⅞" (A)
1 square, 4½" x 4½" (F)

Blue print
4 squares, 3¼" x 3¼" (B)
16 squares, 1½" x 1½" (D)

Aqua print
16 squares, 1⅞" x 1⅞" (C)

Novelty print
4 squares, 2½" x 2½" (E)

INSTRUCTIONS

1. Referring to "Triangle Squares" on page 124, use the teal and white A squares to make four of unit 1. Referring to "Fast Flying Geese" on page 124, use the blue B and aqua C squares to make 16 of unit 2.

Unit 1.
Make 4.

Unit 2.
Make 16.

2. Sew the units and pieces D–F together as shown to complete the block.

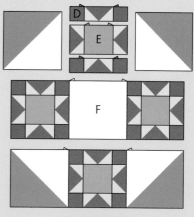

Block assembly

Soldier's Star

Carol Hopkins • carolhopkinsdesigns.com

MATERIALS

Rust print
8 squares, 2⅞" x 2⅞" (A)
4 squares, 4½" x 4½" (B)

Brown print
4 squares, 2⅞" x 2⅞" (A)
1 square, 4½" x 4½" (B)
8 squares, 2½" x 2½" (C)

Cream print
4 squares, 2⅞" x 2⅞" (A)

INSTRUCTIONS

1. Referring to "Triangle Squares" on page 124, pair rust and brown A squares to make eight of unit 1. Pair rust and cream A squares to make eight of unit 2.

Unit 1.
Make 8.

Unit 2.
Make 8.

2. Referring to "Stitch and Flip" on page 124, use the rust B and brown C squares to make four of unit 3.

Unit 3.
Make 4.

3. Sew the units and brown B square together as shown to complete the block.

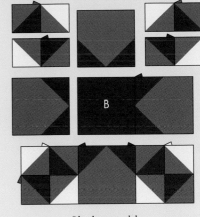

Block assembly

Spectrum Square

Linda Ambrosini

MATERIALS

▧ = Cut in half diagonally.

Assorted light- and medium-value batiks
6 rectangles, 2½" x 12½" (A)
Dark multicolored batik
2 squares, 6⅞" x 6⅞" ▧ (B)

INSTRUCTIONS

1. Sew the A strips together side by side as shown to make a 12½" x 12½" pieced square.

2. Fold the patchwork in half both ways and lightly crease the folds. Using the folds as guides, trim off the corners as shown.

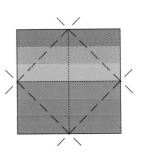

3. Add the B triangles as shown to complete the block.

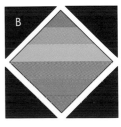

Block assembly

67

Spring Blossom

Peg Spradlin • handicraftsbypeg.com

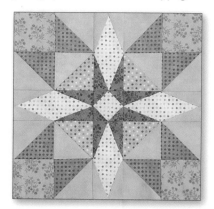

MATERIALS

Patterns are on the enclosed disk.

Cream dotted fabric
1 square, 2½" x 2½" (A)
4 of pattern C

Peach tone-on-tone fabric
4 squares, 1½" x 1½" (B)
4 *each* of patterns D and D reversed

Blue dotted fabric and light-green solid
2 squares, 3⅜" x 3⅜", from *each* fabric (E)

Green dotted fabric
4 squares, 3⅜" x 3⅜" (E)

Light-blue solid
4 *each* of patterns D and D reversed
4 squares, 3⅜" x 3⅜" (E)

Blue tone-on-tone fabric
4 squares, 3" x 3" (F)

INSTRUCTIONS

1. Referring to "Stitch and Flip" on page 124, use the cream A and peach B squares to make the block center.

2. Referring to "Triangle Squares" on page 124, use the blue dotted and light-green E squares to make four of unit 1.

Use the green dotted and light-blue E squares to make eight of unit 2.

Unit 1.
Make 4.

Unit 2.
Make 8.

3. Sew the pieced units and F squares together as shown to complete the block.

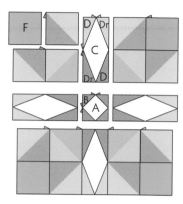

Block assembly

Square and Diamond

Karen Combs • karencombs.com

MATERIALS

▢ = *Cut in half diagonally.*
⊠ = *Cut into quarters diagonally.*

Black-and-lime-green print
1 square, 5⅛" x 5⅛" (A)

Black tone-on-tone fabric
2 squares, 4⅛" x 4⅛" ▢ (B)

Black-on-white print
4 rectangles, 1½" x 7" (C)

Lime-green tone-on-tone fabric
4 squares, 1½" x 1½" (D)
4 squares, 2¼" x 2¼" (E)

White-on-black print
12 squares, 2¼" x 2¼" (E)*

White print
4 squares, 3⅝" x 3⅝" ⊠ (F)
2 squares, 2⅛" x 2⅛" ▢ (G)

**Karen fussy cut the white-on-black E pieces to center the flower motifs.*

INSTRUCTIONS

1. Refering to the block assembly diagram at right, join pieces A–D as shown to make the block center.

2. Join pieces E–G as shown to make four block corners.

3. Sew the pieced corners to the block center to complete the block.

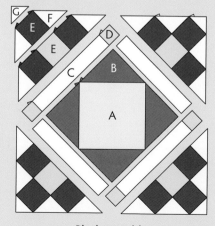

Block assembly

PIECED

Star Across

Laura Blanchard • plumtreequilts.com

MATERIALS

Aqua batik
4 squares, 5" x 5" (A)

Dark-blue batik
8 squares, 3½" x 3½" (B)

Light-purple batik
4 squares, 3½" x 3½" (B)

Light-blue batik
1 square, 3½" x 3½" (B)
8 squares, 2" x 2" (C)

Dark-purple batik
4 rectangles, 2" x 3½" (D)

INSTRUCTIONS

1. Referring to "Stitch and Flip" on page 124, use aqua A and dark-blue B squares to make four of unit 1 as shown.

Unit 1.
Make 4.

2. Use light-purple B and light-blue C squares to make four of unit 2 as shown.

Unit 2.
Make 4.

3. Join the pieced units with the B and D pieces as shown to complete the block.

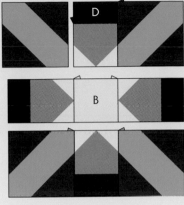

Block assembly

PIECED

Star Checks

Sue Garman • suegarman.blogspot.com

MATERIALS

Assorted red prints
6 squares, 3⅞" x 3⅞" (A)
20 squares, 1½" x 1½" (B)

Cream print
6 squares, 3⅞" x 3⅞" (A)
8 squares, 1½" x 1½" (B)
4 rectangles, 1½" x 2½" (C)

INSTRUCTIONS

1. Referring to "Triangle Squares" on page 124, use the red and cream A squares to make 12 triangle squares.

Make 12.

2. Join the B squares and C rectangles to assemble the center section in rows as shown in the diagram. Join the triangle squares to the center section to complete the block as shown.

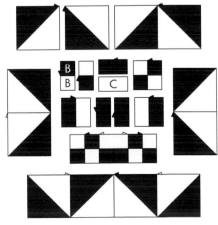

Block assembly

Star Crossover

Diane Nagle • peddlecarquilts.blogspot.com

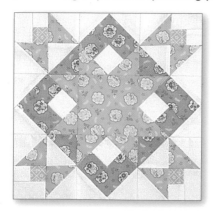

MATERIALS

◻ = Cut in half diagonally.

White tone-on-tone fabric
6 squares, 2⅞" x 2⅞" (A)
4 squares, 1½" x 1½" (B)
4 rectangles, 1½" x 2½" (C)
4 squares, 1⅞" x 1⅞" (D)
4 squares, 2⅞" x 2⅞" ◻ (E)

Blue print
4 squares, 2⅞" x 2⅞" (A)
4 squares, 2⅞" x 2⅞" ◻ (E)
1 square, 4½" x 4½" (G)

Pink print
2 squares, 2⅞" x 2⅞" (A)
4 squares, 1⅞" x 1⅞" (D)
4 rectangles, 1⅞" x 3¼" (F)

Yellow print
4 squares, 1½" x 1½" (B)

INSTRUCTIONS

1. Referring to "Triangle Squares" on page 124, use blue and white A squares to make eight of unit 1. Use pink and white A squares to make four of unit 2.

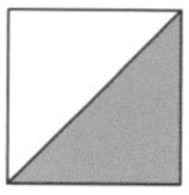

Unit 1.
Make 8.

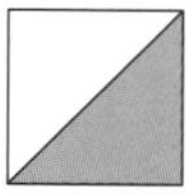

Unit 2.
Make 4.

2. Sew the units together with pieces B–G as shown to complete the block.

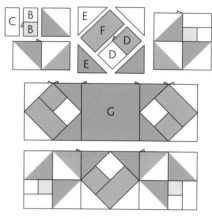

Block assembly

Star Dance

Celine Perkins • perkinsdrygoods.com

MATERIALS

◻ = Cut in half diagonally.
⊠ = Cut into quarters diagonally.

Brown print
1 square, 4½" x 4½" (A)
4 squares, 2½" x 2½" (B)
2 squares, 2⅞" x 2⅞" (E)

Tan print
12 squares, 2½" x 2½" (B)
2 squares, 2⅞" x 2⅞" (E)
1 square, 5¼" x 5¼" ⊠ (D)

Dark-blue print
2 squares, 4⅞" x 4⅞" ◻ (C)

Medium-blue print
1 square, 5¼" x 5¼" ⊠ (D)

INSTRUCTIONS

1. Referring to "Stitch and Flip" on page 124, use the brown A and four tan B squares to make unit 1 as shown.

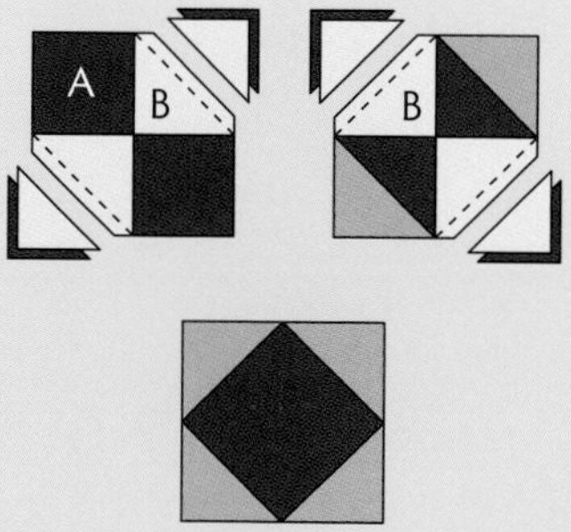

Unit 1.
Make 1.

2. Referring to "Triangle Squares" on page 124, pair the brown and tan E squares to make four of unit 2.

Unit 2.
Make 4.

3. Sew the units and pieces B–D together as shown to complete the block.

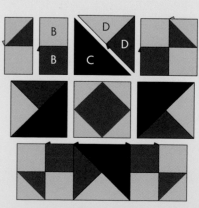

Block assembly

Star Flight

Kathy Brown • the-teachers-pet.com

MATERIALS

Red print
1 square, 4½" x 4½" (A)
4 squares, 2½" x 2½" (B)
1 square, 5¼" x 5¼" (C)

Tan solid
8 squares, 2½" x 2½" (B)
4 rectangles, 2½" x 4½" (E)

Brown print
8 squares, 2½" x 2½" (B)
4 squares, 2⅞" x 2⅞" (D)

INSTRUCTIONS

1. Referring to "Stitch and Flip" on page 124, use the red A and four tan B squares as shown to make unit 1.

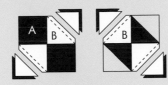

Unit 1.
Make 1.

2. Referring to "Fast Flying Geese" on page 124, use the red C and brown D squares to make four of unit 2.

Unit 2.
Make 4.

3. Sew units 1 and 2 together with the remaining B and E pieces as shown to complete the block.

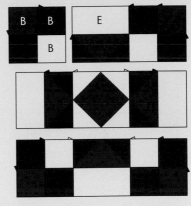

Block assembly

Star-Crossed Love

Scott Hansen • bluenickelstudios.com

MATERIALS

Blue dotted print
1 square, 5¼" x 5¼" (A)
1 square, 2½" x 2½" (C)

White-and-blue plaid
1 square, 5¼" x 5¼" (A)
8 squares, 2⅞" x 2⅞" (B)

Red print
4 squares, 2⅞" x 2⅞" (B)
2 rectangles, 1½" x 2½" (D)
2 rectangles, 1½" x 4½" (E)

Blue print
4 squares, 2⅞" x 2⅞" (B)
4 squares, 2½" x 2½" (C)

White print
4 squares, 2½" x 2½" (C)

INSTRUCTIONS

1. Referring to "Fast Flying Geese" on page 124, use the dotted A and plaid B squares to make four of unit 1. Use the plaid A and red B squares to make four of unit 2.

Unit 1.
Make 4.

Unit 2.
Make 4.

2. Referring to "Triangle Squares" on page 124, use the plaid B squares and blue-print B squares to make eight of unit 3.

Unit 3.
Make 8.

3. Sew units 1–3 together with pieces C–E as shown to complete the block.

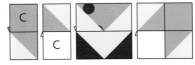

Block assembly

71

Summer Fun

Barbara Groves and Mary Jacobson • meandmysisterdesigns.com

MATERIALS

White dotted fabric
    2 squares, 5¼" x 5¼" (A)
Green plaid
    2 squares, 5¼" x 5¼" (A)
    4 squares, 2½" x 2½" (B)

Pink tone-on-tone fabric
    4 squares, 2½" x 2½" (B)
    4 rectangles, 2½" x 4½" (C)
Blue print
    1 square, 4½" x 4½" (D)

INSTRUCTIONS

1. Referring to "Quarter-Square Triangles" on page 124, pair the white and green A squares to make four units as shown.

Make 4.

2. Join the units with pieces B–D as shown to complete the block.

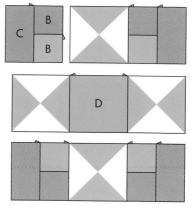

Block assembly

Summer Picnic

Pam Vieira-McGinnis • pamkittymorning.blogspot.com

MATERIALS

Cream print
    6 squares, 2⅞" x 2⅞" (A)
    12 squares, 2½" x 2½" (C)
Red-checked fabric
    6 squares, 2⅞" x 2⅞" (A)
    4 squares, 2½" x 2½" (C)
Blue print
    8 rectangles, 2½" x 4½" (B)
    1 square, 4½" x 4½" (D)

INSTRUCTIONS

1. Referring to "Triangle Squares" on page 124, pair the red and cream A squares to make 12 of unit 1.

Unit 1.
Make 12.

2. Referring to "Stitch and Flip" on page 124, sew cream C squares to blue B pieces as shown to make four each of units 2 and 3. Make one of unit 4 from the red C and blue D squares.

Unit 2.   Unit 3.   Unit 4.
Make 4.   Make 4.   Make 1.

3. Join the units with the remaining cream C squares as shown to complete the block.

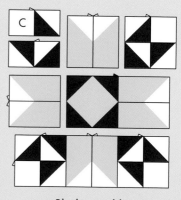

Block assembly

Summer Star

Joanna Figueroa • figtreeandco.com

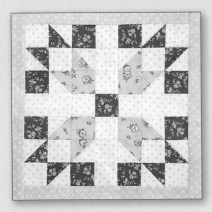

MATERIALS

Red print
4 squares, 2⅜" x 2⅜" (A)
9 squares, 2" x 2" (B)

Cream dotted print
8 squares, 2⅜" x 2⅜" (A)
20 squares, 2" x 2" (B)

Green print
4 squares, 2⅜" x 2⅜" (A)
4 squares, 2" x 2" (B)

Gold dotted print
2 rectangles, 1¼" x 11" (C)
2 rectangles, 1¼" x 12½" (D)

INSTRUCTIONS

1. Referring to "Triangle Squares" on page 124, pair each of the red and green A squares with a cream A square to make eight each of unit 1 and unit 2.

Unit 1.
Make 8.

Unit 2.
Make 8.

2. Referring to the block assembly diagram at right, join units 1 and 2 with the B squares as shown to make the block center.

3. Matching centers and ends, sew the C strips to the block sides. Add the D strips to the top and bottom to complete the block.

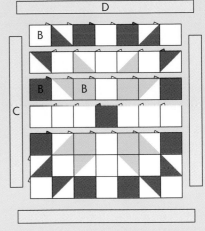

Block assembly

PIECED

Sunburst

Nancy Mahoney • nancymahoney.com

MATERIALS

Patterns are on the enclosed disk.

Purple batik
16 of pattern A
Light-blue batik
16 of pattern B
Beige batik
16 of pattern C
1 square, 12½" x 12½" (E)
Blue-and-purple batik
1 of pattern D

Template plastic
Heavy-weight gold metallic thread

INSTRUCTIONS

1. Referring to "Set-in Seams" on page 124, sew the A and B pieces together as shown. Add the C pieces to make the center unit.

Center unit

2. Prepare D for turned-edge appliqué. Machine zigzag D to the center unit. The center unit should measure 10½". Fold it in half both ways and lightly crease the folds.

3. Fold E in half both ways and lightly crease the folds. Trace a 9½" circle on

the template plastic. Use this template to cut a circle from the center of E to make the block frame. To set the center unit into the frame, align the creases and pin. Add a few more pins between the creases as shown. With the center unit next to the feed dogs, join to complete the block.

E

9½"

Frame

4. Couch metallic thread around D with a machine zigzag stitch.

Block

73

Sunset Fiesta

Judy Laquidara • patchworktimes.com

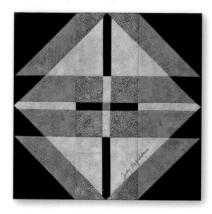

MATERIALS

Black tone-on-tone fabric
 2 squares, 4⅞" x 4⅞" (A)
 4 squares, 2½" x 2½" (B)
 2 rectangles, 1" x 4½" (C)
 2 rectangles, 1" x 2¼" (F)

Teal tone-on-tone fabric
 2 squares, 4⅞" x 4⅞" (A)
 4 rectangles, 2¼" x 4½" (D)
 1 square, 1" x 1" (G)

Yellow tone-on-tone fabric
 4 squares, 2½" x 2½" (B)
 2 rectangles, 1" x 4½" (C)

4 rectangles, 2¼" x 4½" (D)
2 rectangles, 1" x 2¼" (F)

Pink tone-on-tone fabric
 4 squares, 2½" x 2½" (B)
 4 squares, 2¼" x 2¼" (E)

INSTRUCTIONS

1. Referring to "Triangle Squares" on page 124, pair the black and teal A squares to make four triangle squares. Referring to "Stitch and Flip" on page 124, add a yellow B square to each teal corner as shown to complete four of unit 1.

Unit 1.
Make 4.

2. Sew a black C rectangle between two yellow D pieces. Use the stitch-and-flip technique to add pink B squares to the corners as shown, above right, to make two of unit 2. In the same way, use the yellow C, teal D, and black B pieces to make two of unit 3.

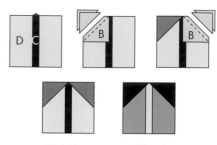

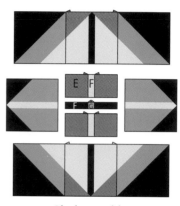

Unit 2.
Make 2.

Unit 3.
Make 2.

3. Join the pieced units with pieces E–G as shown to complete the block.

Block assembly

Sweet Tweets

Angie Hodapp

MATERIALS

Patterns are on the enclosed disk.

Gold dotted fabric
 4 of pattern A

Green print
 4 of pattern B

Beige print
 4 of pattern A

Light-green print
 4 of pattern B

Black print
 1 square, 4½" x 4½" (C)

INSTRUCTIONS

1. Using one each of gold A, green B, beige A, and light-green B, assemble a section as shown. Repeat to make four sections.

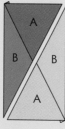

Make 4.

2. Noting the orientation of the sections, sew a section to the bottom of the C square with a partial seam as shown. Sew the remaining sections to the right, top, and left of C. Finish the partial seam to complete the block.

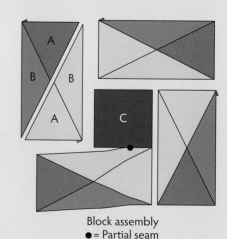

Block assembly
● = Partial seam

Tapestry

Rebecca LoGiudice • willowhillquilts.net

MATERIALS

Dark-red tone-on-tone fabric
1 square, 4½" x 4½" (A)

Red print*
2 rectangles, 1½" x 2½" (B)
4 rectangles, 2½" x 4½" (D)
8 squares, 2½" x 2½" (E)

Medium-red tone-on-tone fabric
2 rectangles, 1½" x 2½" (B)

Gold print
4 rectangles, 2" x 2½" (C)
4 rectangles, 2½" x 4½" (D)
12 squares, 2½" x 2½" (E)
4 rectangles, 2½" x 4" (F)

Becca fussy cut the red-print pieces. You can audition fabric by cutting a "window" in freezer paper the size of the finished piece.

INSTRUCTIONS

1. Referring to "Stitch and Flip" on page 124, sew the gold-print F squares to red-print D rectangles to make four of unit 1 as shown. Sew red-print F squares to gold G pieces to make two each of units 2 and 3 and to gold D pieces to make two each of units 4 and 5.

Unit 1.
Make 4.

Unit 2.
Make 2.

Unit 3.
Make 2.

Unit 4.
Make 2.

Unit 5.
Make 2.

2. Positioning matching red B pieces opposite each other, join pieces A–C with the pieced units as shown to complete the block.

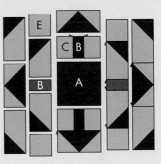

Block assembly

Texas Circle Around

Lynn Roddy Brown • lynnroddybrown.com

MATERIALS

◻ = Cut in half diagonally.

Assorted dark prints
4 squares, 4⅞" x 4⅞" ◻ (B)
(You'll have 4 extra triangles.)
8 rectangles, 1¾" x 4½" (D)

Assorted light prints
1 square, 4½" x 4½" (A)
4 squares, 4⅞" x 4⅞" ◻ (B)
(You'll have 4 extra triangles.)
8 rectangles, 1⅞" x 4½" (C)

INSTRUCTIONS

1. Sew the dark and light B triangles together to make four triangle squares. Save the leftover triangles for another block.

2. Sew the C and D pieces together as shown to make four strip-pieced units.

3. Join the strip-pieced units, the triangle squares, and the A square as shown to complete the block.

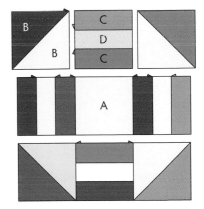

Block assembly

Tile Works

Monique Dillard • opengatequilts.com

MATERIALS

Black print
4 squares, 2⅞" x 2⅞" (A)
1 square, 5¼" x 5¼" (B)
4 squares, 2½" x 2½" (C)
Beige tone-on-tone fabric
8 squares, 2⅞" x 2⅞" (A)
4 squares, 2½" x 2½" (C)
1 square, 4½" x 4½" (D)

Red tone-on-tone fabric
4 squares, 2⅞" x 2⅞" (A)
1 square, 5¼" x 5¼" (B)

INSTRUCTIONS

1. Referring to "Triangle Squares" on page 124, pair the black and beige A squares to make eight of unit 1.

Unit 1.
Make 8.

2. Referring to "Fast Flying Geese" on page 124, sew the red A squares to the black B pieces to make four of unit 2. Sew the beige A squares to the red B pieces to make four of unit 3.

Unit 2.
Make 4.

Unit 3.
Make 4.

3. Join the pieced units with the C and D squares as shown to complete the block.

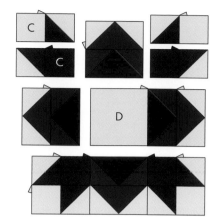

Block assembly

Tulip Twist

Deanne Eisenman • snugglesquilts.com

MATERIALS

Light-blue tone-on-tone fabric
4 squares, 2⅜" x 2⅜" (A)
8 squares, 1½" x 1½" (C)
4 rectangles, 2" x 2½" (F)
4 rectangles, 2" x 4" (G)
Purple print
4 squares, 2⅜" x 2⅜" (A)
4 rectangles, 2" x 2½" (F)
Green tone-on-tone fabric
4 rectangles, 1½" x 6½" (B)
4 rectangles, 1½" x 5½" (D)

Purple tone-on-tone fabric
4 squares, 1½" x 1½" (C)
Dark-blue tone-on-tone fabric
4 squares, 2½" x 2½" (E)
Aqua print
4 rectangles, 2" x 4" (G)

INSTRUCTIONS

1. Referring to "Triangle Squares" on page 124, join the A squares to make eight of unit 1.

2. Referring to "Stitch and Flip" on page 124, sew the light-blue and purple C squares to the green B pieces, noting color placement, to make four of unit 2. Sew a light-blue C square to the D pieces as shown to make four of unit 3.

Unit 2.
Make 4.

3. Join units 1–3 with pieces E–G to make four sections as shown. Sew the sections together to complete the block.

Unit 3.
Make 4.

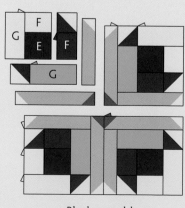

Block assembly

Tumbler Star

Benita Skinner • victorianaquiltdesigns.com

MATERIALS

⬜ = Cut in half diagonally.
⊠ = Cut into quarters diagonally.

White tone-on-tone fabric
 1 square, 5¼" x 5¼" ⊠ (A)
 4 squares, 4½" x 4½" (C)
Medium-purple tone-on-tone fabric
 1 square, 5¼" x 5¼" ⊠ (A)
 1 square, 4⅞" x 4⅞" ⬜ (B)
Dark-purple tone-on-tone fabric
 1 square, 5¼" x 5¼" ⊠ (A)
 1 square, 4⅞" x 4⅞" ⬜ (B)

INSTRUCTIONS

1. Join white and medium-purple A triangles as shown; sew a dark-purple B triangle to each pair to make unit 1. In the same manner, join white and dark-purple A triangles with a medium-purple B triangle to make unit 2. Make two of each unit.

Unit 1.
Make 2.

Unit 2.
Make 2.

2. Join dark-purple and medium-purple A triangles to make one of unit 3.

Unit 3.
Make 1.

3. Join units 1–3 with the C squares as shown to complete the block.

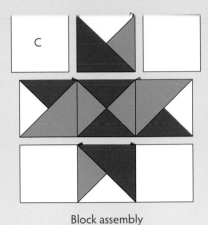

Block assembly

Twist and Shout

Chris Hoover • whirligigdesigns.com

MATERIALS

Pattern is on the enclosed disk.

⬜ = Cut in half diagonally.

Green print and red print
From *each*:
 1 square, 2⅞" x 2⅞" (A)
 1 square, 3¾" x 3¾" ⬜ (C)
  (You'll have 1 extra triangle from each fabric.)
 1 rectangle, 3⅜" x 12" (D)

Cream print
 1 square, 2⅞" x 2⅞" (A)*
Cream tone-on-tone fabric
 2 *each* of patterns B and B reversed

Chris fussy cut the cream A square to center the mistletoe motif.

INSTRUCTIONS

1. Referring to the block assembly diagram at right, sew the A squares together as shown.

2. Using a partial seam, sew a B reversed piece to the green A square as shown. In a counterclockwise direction, join the red D rectangle, B reversed piece, and green D rectangle to the A squares. Complete the partial seam.

3. Join the B and C triangles and complete the block as shown.

4. Trim the corners from the D pieces as shown.

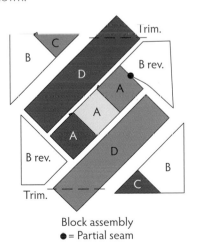

Block assembly
● = Partial seam

Upcycle

Karen Griska • onlinequiltmuseum.com

PIECED

MATERIALS

Teal solid
    4 squares, 5¼" x 5¼" (A)

Selvages
    1⅛"-wide strips to total about 100"
       (see "Instructions" at right)
    2 strips, 1⅛" x 10" (B)
    4 strips, 1⅛" x 11¼" (C)
    2 strips, 1⅛" x 12½" (D)

INSTRUCTIONS

1. Cut the selvage strips about 1⅛" wide and anywhere from 2" to 8" long. (Adding extra length will give you more room to position the words and color windows wherever you like.)

2. Fold an A square in half diagonally and gently crease the fold. With the right side up, lay the first selvage strip ¼" from the fold as shown. Sew along the bound edge of the strip (not the raw edge). Lay the next strip right side up along the first strip, covering the raw edge of the first strip with the bound edge of the second strip; sew along the bound edge. Keep adding and sewing strips to cover half of A as shown. Trim the strips even with the edges of A to complete the unit. Make four units.

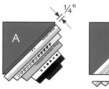

Make 4.

3. Join the four units as shown. On one side of the joined units, lay the bound edge of a B strip over the ¼" seam allowance, matching the centers and ends. Sew along the bound edge of B. Repeat to add the second B strip to the opposite side. Add the C and D strips in the same way. Center and trim the block to 12½" x 12½".

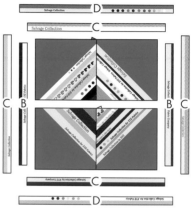

Block assembly

Ups and Downs

Camille Roskelley • thimbleblossoms.com

MATERIALS

Natural muslin
    8 squares, 3⅞" x 3⅞"

4 red prints
    1 square, 3⅞" x 3⅞", from *each* fabric

4 blue prints
    1 square, 3⅞" x 3⅞", from *each* fabric

INSTRUCTIONS

1. Referring to "Triangle Squares" on page 124, pair each red and blue square with a muslin square to make 16 triangle squares.

Make 8.   Make 8.

2. Noting color placement, sew the triangle squares together as shown to complete the block.

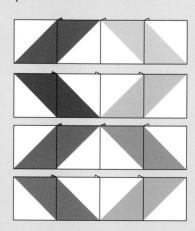

Block assembly

78

Vanishing Squares

Sandi Irish • irishchain.com

MATERIALS

◻ = Cut in half diagonally.

Red-orange batiks and green batiks
From *each* color group:
- 1 square, 2⅞" x 2⅞" ◻ (A) (You'll have 1 extra triangle from each color group.)
- 1 rectangle, 1½" x 2½" (B)
- 1 rectangle, 2½" x 3½" (D)
- 1 rectangle, 3½" x 5½" (F)
- 1 rectangle, 4½" x 8½" (H)

Black batik
- 1 square, 1½" x 1½" (C)
- 2 squares, 2½" x 2½" (E)
- 1 square, 3½" x 3½" (G)
- 1 rectangle, 2½" x 4½" (I)

Blue batik
- 1 square, 2½" x 2½" (E)

INSTRUCTIONS

1. Sew a green and a red-orange A triangle together to make a triangle square.

2. Add pieces B-I as shown to complete the block.

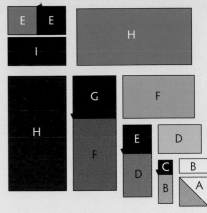

Block assembly

What's the Point?

Sherri Driver • mccallsquilting.com

MATERIALS

Yellow print
- 4 squares, 4½" x 4½" (A)

Brown print
- 16 squares, 2½" x 2½" (B)

Green-striped fabric
- 8 rectangles, 2½" x 4½" (C) (see "Instructions" at right)

Green print
- 1 square, 4½" x 4½" (A)

Template plastic
- 1 rectangle, 2½" x 4½" (C)

INSTRUCTIONS

1. Mark the stripe placement on the template as a guide to cutting mirror-image C pieces as shown. Cut four with the stripe running diagonally in one direction and four with the stripe running diagonally in the opposite direction.

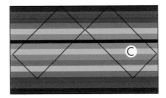

2. Referring to "Stitch and Flip" on page 124, sew brown B squares to opposite corners of yellow A squares to make four of unit 1.

Unit 1.
Make 4.

3. Noting the direction of the stripe, sew brown B squares to the C pieces to make four each of units 2 and 3.

Unit 2.
Make 4.

Unit 3.
Make 4.

4. Join the pieced units with the green A square as shown to complete the block.

Block assembly

79

Wild Blue Yonder

Scott Murkin • patchworkpossibilities.com

Dark-blue striped fabric
  4 rectangles, 2⅝" x 4¾" (A)
Dark-blue tone-on-tone fabric
  2 squares, 3⅞" x 3⅞" ◻ (B)
  2 squares, 4¼" x 4¼" ⊠ (C)

INSTRUCTIONS

1. Sew the dark and light A rectangles together side by side in pairs. Make four.

2. Sew the dark and light C triangles together along short edges as shown to make eight pairs.

3. Sew the C units and B triangles to the A units. Make four. Join the sections as shown to complete the block.

Block assembly

MATERIALS

◻ = *Cut in half diagonally.*
⊠ = *Cut into quarters diagonally.*

Light-blue tone-on-tone fabric
  4 rectangles, 2⅝" x 4¾" (A)
  2 squares, 3⅞" x 3⅞" ◻ (B)
  2 squares, 4¼" x 4¼" ⊠ (C)

Wishing Star

Bonnie Mitchell

Cream print #2
  2 rectangles, ⅞" x 4⅝" (D)
  2 rectangles, ⅞" x 5⅜" (E)
Pink print
  2 rectangles, 1¼" x 5⅜" (F)
  2 rectangles, 1¼" x 6⅞" (G)
Green print
  1 square, 3⅜" x 3⅜" ⊠ (I)

INSTRUCTIONS

1. Referring to "Stitch and Flip" on page 124, sew the red B squares to the cream A rectangles to make four each of units 1 and 2 as shown.

2. Sew the units and pieces C–J together as shown to complete the block.

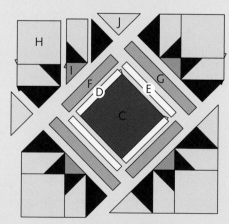

Block assembly

MATERIALS

⊠ = *Cut into quarters diagonally.*

Cream print #1
  8 rectangles, 2" x 3½" (A)
  4 squares, 3½" x 3½" (H)
  1 square, 4¼" x 4¼" ⊠ (J)
Red tone-on-tone fabric
  8 squares, 2" x 2" (B)
  2 squares, 4¼" x 4¼" ⊠ (J)
Red print
  1 square, 4⅝" x 4⅝" (C)

Unit 1.
Make 4.

Unit 2.
Make 4.

Foundation-Pieced
BLOCKS

FOUNDATION-PIECED

Art Deco Star

Susan Cook • larkspurlanedesigns.com

MATERIALS

Foundation patterns are on the enclosed disk.

Medium-light-purple tone-on-tone fabric
Section 1: piece 1
Section 2: piece 1

Black solid
Section 1: pieces 2, 4, and 5
Section 2: piece 2
Section 3: pieces 2 and 3

Medium-dark-purple tone-on-tone fabric
Section 1: piece 3
Section 3: piece 1

Light-purple tone-on-tone fabric
Section 2: piece 3

Gold tone-on-tone fabric
Section 4: piece 1

Dark-purple tone-on-tone fabric
Section 4: piece 2

INSTRUCTIONS

1. Each quadrant of the block is made from four sections. Make four paper copies *each* of foundation sections 1–4.

2. Foundation piece the sections in numerical order, pressing and trimming after each piece addition. Refer to the block assembly diagram and join sections 1–4 as shown to make the quadrants. Join the quadrants as shown to complete the block.

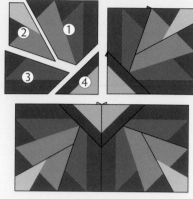

Block assembly

Happiness in a Block

Teresa Fields

MATERIALS

Foundation pattern is on the enclosed disk.

Bright-green tone-on-tone fabric
Pieces 3 and 4

Bright-pink tone-on-tone fabric
Piece 1

Bright-blue tone-on-tone fabric
Piece 2

Bright multicolored print
Piece 5

INSTRUCTIONS

1. The block is made from four quadrants. Make four paper copies of the foundation.

2. Foundation piece the quadrants in numerical order, pressing and trimming after each piece addition. Join the quadrants as shown to complete the block.

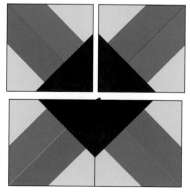

Block assembly

Hot Fudge Please

Julie Pieri • quiltedpleasures.com

MATERIALS

Foundation patterns are on the enclosed disk.

◻ = *Cut in half diagonally.*

Cream batik
Section 1: pieces 1, 3, 5, 7, 9, 11, and 13
5 squares, 2⅞" x 2⅞" ◻ (A)
(You'll have 1 extra triangle.)

Dark-brown batik
Section 1: pieces 2, 4, 6, 8, 10, and 12
4 squares, 2⅞" x 2⅞" ◻ (A)

Teal batik
Sections 2 and 3: pieces 1, 3, 5, and 7
1 square, 2⅞" x 2⅞" ◻ (A)

Blue batik
Sections 2 and 3: pieces 2, 4, 6, and 8

Red batik
1 square, 2⅞" x 2⅞" ◻ (A)
(You'll have 1 extra triangle.)

Aqua batik
1 square, 2⅞" x 2⅞" ◻ (A)
2 rectangles, 2½" x 8½" (B)
1 square, 2½" x 2½" (C)

INSTRUCTIONS

1. Make paper copies of foundation sections 1, 2, and 3. Foundation piece the sections in numerical order, pressing and trimming after each piece addition.

2. Join the foundation-pieced sections and pieces A–C as shown to complete the block.

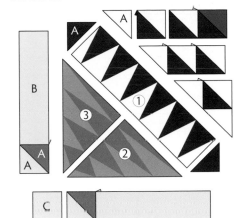

Block assembly

Ice Crystal

Eileen Fowler • quiltmaker.com

MATERIALS

Foundation patterns are on the enclosed disk.

Medium-blue print #1
Sections 1, 2, and 3: pieces 1 and 12
Dark-blue batik #1
Sections 1, 2, and 3: pieces 2, 3, 5, 7, 13, and 14
Medium-blue print #2
Sections 1, 2, and 3: pieces 4 and 8
White print
Sections 1, 2, and 3: pieces 6 and 10
Dark-blue batik #2
Sections 1, 2, and 3: pieces 9 and 11

INSTRUCTIONS

1. Each half of the block is made from three sections. Make two paper copies *each* of foundation sections 1, 2, and 3. Foundation piece the sections in numerical order, pressing and trimming after each piece addition.

2. Join sections 1–3 as shown to make each block half. To reduce bulk, press the seams open. Join the block halves to complete the block.

Section 1. Make 2.   Section 2. Make 2.   Section 3. Make 2.

Block assembly

Isobel's Flight

Cinzia White • cinziawhite.com

MATERIALS

Patterns are on the enclosed disk.

Blue tone-on-tone fabric
Sections 1 and 2: pieces 1, 4, 7, 10, 13, and 16
2 of pattern B

White print
Sections 1 and 2: pieces 2, 3, 5, 6, 8, 9, 11, 12, 14, 15, 17, and 18
1 of pattern A
2 of pattern B

INSTRUCTIONS

1. Make a paper copy of foundation sections 1 and 2. Foundation piece the sections in numerical order, pressing and trimming after each piece addition.

2. Referring to "Curved Piecing" on page 123, join the foundation sections with the A and B pieces as shown to complete the block.

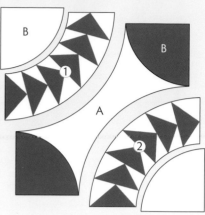

Block assembly

Midnight Dream

Carolyn Cullinan McCormick • addaquarter.com

MATERIALS

Foundation patterns are on the enclosed disk.

Cream tone-on-tone fabric
Section 1: pieces 1 and 7
Section 2: pieces 4 and 5
Section 3: pieces 2–5

Light-purple batik
Section 1: pieces 2, 3, and 8
Section 2: pieces 2 and 3
Section 3: piece 1

Dark-purple batik
Section 1: pieces 4–6
Section 2: piece 1

INSTRUCTIONS

1. Make four paper copies of foundation sections 1 and 2 and one copy of foundation section 3. Foundation piece each section in numerical order, pressing and trimming after each piece addition.

2. Join the sections as shown to complete the block.

Block assembly

Section 1. Make 4.

Section 2. Make 4.

Section 3. Make 1.

Midnight Garden

Carol Doak • caroldoak.com

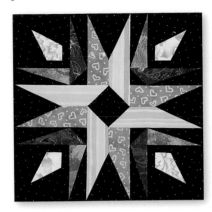

MATERIALS

Foundation pattern is on the enclosed disk.

Yellow tone-on-tone fabric
Piece 1
Black print
Pieces 2–5, 8–10, and 13–15

Light-pink tone-on-tone fabric
Piece 6
Pink print
Piece 7
Green print
Piece 11
Light-green tone-on-tone fabric
Piece 12

INSTRUCTIONS

1. The block is made from four identical sections. Make four paper copies of the foundation. Foundation piece the sections in numerical order, pressing and trimming after each piece addition.

2. Join the sections as shown to complete the block.

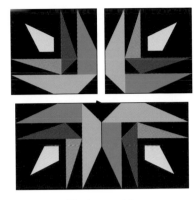

Block assembly

Nova

Angie Hodapp

MATERIALS

Foundation patterns are on the enclosed disk.

Multicolored print
Section 1: piece 1
Brown tone-on-tone fabric
Section 1: pieces 2–5
Section 2: piece 2
Yellow tone-on-tone fabric
Section 2: pieces 1 and 3
Green tone-on-tone fabric
Section 3: piece 1

Coral tone-on-tone fabric
Section 3: piece 2
Section 4: piece 4
Dark-teal tone-on-tone fabric
Section 4: piece 2
Section 5: piece 1
Medium-teal tone-on-tone fabric
Section 4: piece 3
Section 5: piece 2
Brown print
Section 4: piece 1
Section 5: piece 3

INSTRUCTIONS

1. Make one paper copy of foundation section 1 and four paper copies *each* of sections 2–5. Foundation piece each section in numerical order, pressing and trimming after each piece addition.

Section 1.   Section 2.   Section 3.
Make 1.   Make 4.   Make 4.

Section 4.   Section 5.
Make 4.   Make 4.

2. Add the section 2 pieces to section 1, pressing after each addition. Repeat to add the section 3 pieces. Join sections 4 and 5 in pairs. Add a section 4/5 to the block center with a partial seam as shown. Add the remaining 4/5 sections, working counterclockwise. Finish the partial seam to complete the block.

 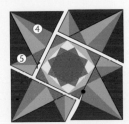

Block assembly
● = Partial seam

Pinwheel O'Strings

Rachel Griffith · psiquilt.com

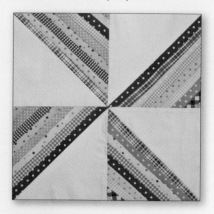

MATERIALS

Assorted prints
    2 strips, 2" x 10"
    1"-wide strips to total 180"
White tone-on-tone fabric
    2 squares, 6⅞" x 6⅞"
Foundation paper
    2 squares, 6⅞" x 6⅞"

INSTRUCTIONS

1. Lay a 2" x 10" strip, right side up, diagonally across the center of a foundation-paper square. Aligning raw edges, lay a 1" strip, right side down, on the center strip as shown. Sew through all the layers ¼" from the raw edges of the strips. Press the top strip open.

Section piecing

2. Continue adding 1" strips from the center outward in both directions until the entire foundation has been covered.

Trim the fabric even with the paper. Repeat to make two units.

Make 2.

3. Using the "Triangle Squares" technique on page 124, pair a white fabric square with each foundation-pieced square, sewing in the same direction as the strips, to make four triangle squares. Join them as shown to complete the block.

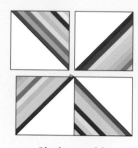

Block assembly

Shoe Boxes

Denise Starck · quiltmaker.com

MATERIALS

Foundation patterns are on the enclosed disk.

Cream dotted fabric
    2 rectangles, 1¼" x 4¾" (A)
    1 rectangle, 1½" x 11¼" (B)
    2 rectangles, 1⅛" x 10" (C)
    2 rectangles, 1¾" x 12½" (D)
    Sections 1 and 1 reversed: pieces 1, 4, and 5

    Sections 2 and 2 reversed: pieces 2 and 3
    Sections 3 and 3 reversed: pieces 1 and 4

Green print and red print
From *each*:
    Sections 1 and 1 reversed: pieces 2 and 3
    Sections 2 and 2 reversed: piece 1
    Sections 3 and 3 reversed: pieces 2 and 3

INSTRUCTIONS

1. Each shoe is made from three sections. Make two paper copies of *each* foundation and reversed-foundation section.

2. Make one shoe and one reversed shoe from each color. Foundation piece the sections in numerical order, pressing

and trimming after each piece addition. Join the sections to make each shoe.

Make 1 and 1 reversed of each color.

3. Join the shoes with pieces A–D as shown to complete the block.

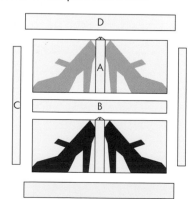

Block assembly

Spiked Pinwheels

Robin Koehler • nestlingsbyrobin.com

MATERIALS

Foundation pattern is on the enclosed disk.

Dark-green batik
Piece 1
Orange batik
Pieces 2 and 4
Dark-rust batik
Pieces 3, 6, and 7
Light-green batik
Piece 5
Brown tone-on-tone fabric
Piece 8
Tan batik
Piece 9

INSTRUCTIONS

1. Make four paper copies of the foundation pattern. Foundation piece each section in numerical order, pressing and trimming after each piece addition.

Make 4.

2. Join the sections as shown to complete the block.

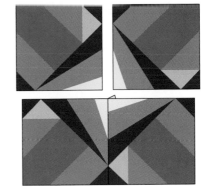

Block assembly

Stars upon Stars

Joen Wolfrom • jwdpublishing.com

MATERIALS

Foundation patterns are on the enclosed disk.

Rust tone-on-tone fabric
Piece 1
Beige tone-on-tone fabric
Pieces 2, 4, and 6
Medium multicolored print
Piece 3
Dark multicolored print
Piece 5

INSTRUCTIONS

1. Each quarter of the block is made from a section 1 and mirror-image section 2. Make four paper copies *each* of foundations 1 and 2. Foundation piece the sections in numerical order, pressing with a dry iron and trimming after each piece addition.

2. Join sections 1 and 2 together in pairs to make four quadrants. Join the quadrants as shown to complete the block.

Block assembly

Swedish Log Cabin

Lorraine Olsen • lorraineolsenquilts.com

MATERIALS

Foundation pattern is on the enclosed disk.

Assorted black prints
  Piece 1
Assorted cream and white prints
  Pieces 2–5

Assorted red prints
  Pieces 6–9
Assorted pink prints
  Pieces 10 and 11
Black solid
  Pieces 12 and 13

INSTRUCTIONS

1. Make four paper copies of the foundation pattern. Foundation piece each section in numerical order, pressing and trimming after each piece addition.

2. Join the sections as shown to complete the block.

Block assembly

Timber

Kay Gentry • nobleneedle.com

MATERIALS

◻ = *Cut in half diagonally.*
⊠ = *Cut into quarters diagonally.*

Assorted prints and tone-on-tone fabrics
  Assorted strips, ½" to 1½" wide x 14"*

Brown tone-on-tone fabric
  4 squares, 2⅞" x 2⅞" ◻ (B)
  1 square, 5¼" x 5¼" ⊠ (D)
  2 squares, 3⅜" x 3⅜" ◻ (F)

Muslin
  1 rectangle, 13" x 20"

Angle or taper strips if desired so piecing will have a random, scrappy look.

INSTRUCTIONS

1. Align the first strip on the left end of the muslin rectangle, right side up. Place the second strip on the first strip, right sides together and aligning the raw edges. Sew through both strips and the muslin foundation with a ¼" seam allowance. Flip the second strip open and press. Continue to add strips randomly across the muslin as shown, pressing the strips open after each addition. Trim the strips even with the edges of the muslin.

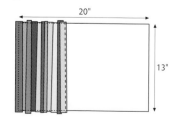

2. From the strip-pieced foundation, cut one strip, 2½" x 20", and two strips, 3" x 20". Cut the 2½" strip into four C pieces, 2½" x 4½". Referring to the cutting diagram, cut the 3" strips into four E pieces, 3" x 9¾", and trim off 3" triangles as shown. From the remaining strip-pieced foundation, cut one A square, 3⅜" x 3⅜".

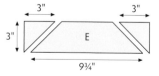

Cutting diagram

3. Assemble the block as shown.

Block assembly

Twirling Star

Nancy Mahoney • nancymahoney.com

MATERIALS

Patterns are on the enclosed disk.

Assorted pink prints
Piece 1
Natural muslin
Pieces 2 and 4

Assorted green prints
Piece 3
Yellow print
1 of pattern A

INSTRUCTIONS

1. Make four paper copies of *each* foundation section. Foundation piece each section in numerical order, pressing and trimming after each piece addition. Notice that Nancy used a dark pink and green for section 1 and light pink and green in section 2.

2. Join sections 1 and 2 in pairs to make four quadrants. Join the quadrants as shown to complete the block.

3. Prepare A for turned-edge appliqué. Using a blind stitch, appliqué A to the center of the block as shown in the photo.

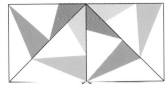

Block assembly.
Appliqué piece A after assembling the block.

Versailles

Chloe Anderson and Colleen Reale • toadusew.com

MATERIALS

Foundation patterns are on the enclosed disk.

Red print
Section 1: piece 1
1 square, 3½" x 3½" (A)
Dark-green print
Section 1: pieces 2 and 3
Sections 2 and 2 reversed: piece 1

Gold tone-on-tone fabric
Section 1: pieces 4 and 5
4 squares, 2" x 2" (B)
Cream print
Sections 2 and 2 reversed: pieces 2 and 4
Medium-green print
Sections 2 and 2 reversed: piece 3

INSTRUCTIONS

1. Referring to "Stitch and Flip" on page 124, sew the gold B squares to the red A square to make the block center.

Make 1.

2. Make four paper copies of foundation section 1 and two copies *each* of foundation sections 2 and 2 reversed. Foundation piece the sections in numerical order, pressing and trimming after each piece addition.

 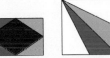

Section 1.
Make 4.

Section 2.
Make 2.

Section 2 reversed.
Make 2.

3. Join the pieced sections as shown to complete the block.

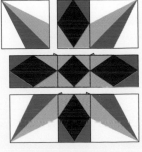

Block assembly

Mixed-Media BLOCKS

Allemande

Sue Daley • busyfingerspatchwork.com

MATERIALS

Foundation patterns are on the enclosed disk.

English paper pieces
    Precut paper pieces for 1" squares (A) and 2", 45° diamonds (B) **OR** medium-weight paper
Yellow tone-on-tone fabric and green-print
    16 of pattern A from *each* fabric
Coral print
    16 of pattern B*

Cream solid
    1 square, 13½" x 13½" (C)
Template plastic

Fussy cut matching B pieces, if desired, as in the block shown.

INSTRUCTIONS

1. If you haven't purchased precut foundation pieces, make your own from the patterns provided on the enclosed disk. Following the instructions for English paper piecing on page 123, baste the A and B pieces to the paper templates and hand sew them together as shown.

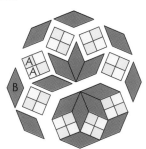

Block assembly

2. Fold piece C in half both ways and lightly crease. Use the creases to position the paper-pieced unit as shown in the appliqué placement diagram. Use matching thread and a hand blind stitch to appliqué the design onto C. Centering the design, trim the block to 12½" x 12½".

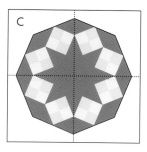

Appliqué placement

American Beauty

Jo Moury

MATERIALS

Appliqué patterns are on the enclosed disk.

◻ = Cut in half diagonally.
⊠ = Cut into quarters diagonally.

Blue plaid and red solid
    2 squares, 3⅞" x 3⅞", from *each* fabric (A)
Red print
    2 squares, 3" x 3" (B)

Dark-blue tone-on-tone fabric
    2 squares, 3" x 3" (B)
    2 squares, 4¼" x 4¼" ⊠ (C)
Cream-with-red print
    4 squares, 3⅞" x 3⅞" ◻ (D)
Cream tone-on-tone fabric
    1 square, 6½" x 6½" (E)
Green tone-on-tone fabric
    ⅜"-wide bias strips for stems
Assorted red, blue, and green prints
    1 set of appliqué pieces
Red tone-on-tone fabric
    5 circles for stuffed berries (F)
Embroidery floss: Green
Fiberfill

INSTRUCTIONS

1. Referring to "Triangle Squares" on page 124, use A squares to make four large triangle-square units and B squares to make four small units as shown.

Make 4.   Make 4.

2. Join the triangle squares with pieces C–E to complete the pieced block.

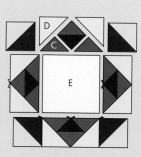

Block assembly

3. Prepare the appliqué pieces for turned-edge appliqué. Refer to "Narrow Bias Stems" on page 123 to prepare the stems. Fold the block in half both ways; lightly crease. Arrange the stems and pieces, and use matching thread and a blind stitch to appliqué them in place.

4. To make the berries, follow the instructions for yo-yos on page 125, but do not turn under ¼" before basting. Insert a small amount of fiberfill into each berry; then pull the threads to gather. Tack the berries in place. Use the green floss and a lazy daisy stitch to embroider leaves.

Bloom Around

Bonnie Olaveson • cottonway.com

MATERIALS

Appliqué patterns are on the enclosed disk.

▢ = *Cut in half diagonally.*

Beige tone-on-tone fabric
  1 square, 9½" x 9½" (A)
  2 squares, 7¼" x 7¼" ▢ (E)

Red tone-on-tone fabric
  1 of pattern B
  4 of pattern C
Blue print
  4 of pattern D
Rickrack: 4 pieces, 8½" long, of red
Fusible web

INSTRUCTIONS

1. Prepare pieces B–D for fusible appliqué.

2. Fold A in half diagonally both ways and lightly crease the folds. Referring to the diagram and using the creases as a guide, position and fuse B–D in alphabetical order to A. Use red thread and a blanket stitch (page 126) to sew around all of the appliqués. Centering the appliqué, trim A to 8½" x 8½".

3. Sew red rickrack to each side of A as shown. Add the E triangles as shown to complete the block.

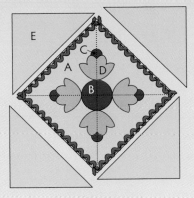

Block assembly and appliqué placement

Blooming Spring

Carrie Quinn and Katie Reed • piecefulgathering.com

MATERIALS

Appliqué patterns are on the enclosed disk.

⊠ = *Cut into quarters diagonally.*

Tan plaid
  2 squares, 4" x 4" ⊠ (A)
  2 rectangles, 3½" x 6½" (D)
  2 rectangles, 3½" x 12½" (E)
Green plaid
  4 rectangles, 1" x 2⅝" (B)
Red plaid
  1 square, 4¾" x 4¾" (C)

Green wool
  4 *each* of patterns F and F reversed
Dark-red wool
  4 of pattern G
Yellow wool
  4 of pattern H
Pink wool
  4 of pattern I
Fusible web
Pearl cotton: dark-red, yellow, pink

INSTRUCTIONS

1. Sew a tan A triangle to either side of each green B piece to make four pieced triangles.

Make 4.

2. Sew the pieced triangles to the C square, and then add the D and E pieces as shown above right to make the block.

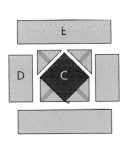

Block assembly

3. Prepare pieces F–I for fusible appliqué. Referring to the appliqué placement diagram, arrange the appliqués on the block; fuse in alphabetical order. Hand blanket stitch (page 126) around each appliqué using matching thread.

Appliqué placement

Bluebirds Welcome

Suzanne McNeill • d-originals.com

MATERIALS

Appliqué patterns are on the enclosed disk.

Cream dotted print
- 2 squares, 2½" x 2½" (A)
- 1 rectangle, 6½" x 8½" (D)
- 2 rectangles, 2½" x 12½" (E)

Brown tone-on-tone fabric
- 1 rectangle, 2½" x 4½" (B)
- 1 rectangle, 4½" x 8½" (C)

Assorted red, blue, green, and gold tone-on-tone fabrics
- 1 *each* of patterns F–H reversed
- 8 of pattern I
- 11 of pattern J

Fusible web

Pearl cotton in assorted colors

INSTRUCTIONS

1. Join pieces A–E as shown to piece the block.

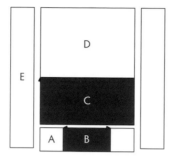

Block assembly

2. Prepare pieces F–J for fusible appliqué. Arrange the appliqués on the block as shown and fuse in place. Using thread to match, machine blanket-stitch (page 126) around each appliqué.

Appliqué placement

3. Referring to the detail photo below, use pearl cotton to add details with a running stitch. Make French-knot eyes.

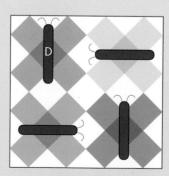

Born to Fly

Lori Smith • frommyhearttoyourhands.com

MATERIALS

Appliqué pattern is on the enclosed disk.

◻ = *Cut in half diagonally.*

⊠ = *Cut into quarters diagonally.*

Natural muslin
- 2 squares, 2⅜" x 2⅜" ◻ (A)
- 3 squares, 4¼" x 4¼" ⊠ (B)
- 5 squares, 2⅝" x 2⅝" (C)

Pink, yellow, teal, and purple prints
- 4 squares, 2⅝" x 2⅝", from *each* fabric (C)

Pink, yellow, teal, and purple solids
- 1 square, 2⅝" x 2⅝", from *each* fabric (C)

Black print
- 4 of pattern D

Fusible web

Embroidery floss: Black

INSTRUCTIONS

1. Join pieces A–C as shown to piece the block.

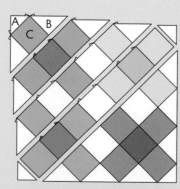

Block assembly

2. Prepare the D pieces for fusible appliqué; fuse as shown to make each butterfly.

3. Referring to the stitches on page 126, use a blanket stitch and the black floss to stitch around each appliqué. Use an outline stitch to embroider the antennae, adding a French knot at each end.

Appliqué and embroidery placement

Butterfly Jungle

Mickey Charleston

MATERIALS

Foundation patterns are on the enclosed disk.

Orange batik
Sections 1 and 1 reversed: piece 1
Section 2: piece 1
Section 3: piece 1

Green batik
Sections 1 and 1 reversed: piece 2

Blue batik
Sections 1 and 1 reversed: piece 3

Gold batik
Sections 1 and 1 reversed: piece 4
Section 2: pieces 2 and 3
Section 3: pieces 2 and 3
1 rectangle, 1⅝" x 4" (B)
1 rectangle, 4" x 5⅛" (C)

Black batik
Section 2: piece 4
1 square, 1⅝" x 1⅝" (A)

Brown-and-black batik
4 rectangles, 3¾" x 10" (D)

INSTRUCTIONS

1. Make one paper copy *each* of foundation sections 1–3 and 1 reversed. Foundation piece the sections in numerical order, pressing and trimming after each piece addition.

Section 1. Make 1 and 1 reversed.

Section 2. Make 1.

Section 3. Make 1.

2. Join pieces A–D with the foundation-pieced sections as shown.

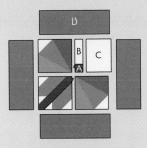

Block assembly

3. Using a 12½" square ruler, trim the block to 12½" x 12½" as shown.

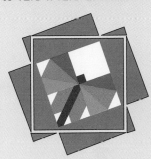

Trim to 12½" x 12½".

Cathedral View

Dana Jones • quiltersnewsletter.com

MATERIALS

Foundation patterns are on the enclosed disk.

Light-orange batik
1 square, 3½" x 3½" (A)

Black solid
2 rectangles, ¾" x 3½" (B)
2 rectangles, ¾" x 4" (C)
2 rectangles, ¾" x 5" (F)
2 rectangles, ¾" x 5½" (G)
2 rectangles, ¾" x 8½" (H)
2 rectangles, ¾" x 9" (I)

Section 1: pieces 2 and 3
Section 2: pieces 2, 3, and 6

Rust batik #1
2 rectangles, 1" x 4" (D)
2 rectangles, 1" x 5" (E)
Section 2: piece 1

Light-green batik #1
Section 1: piece 1

Light-green batik #2
Section 1: piece 4

Dark-green batik #1
Section 1: piece 5

Dark-green batik #2
Section 2: pieces 4 and 5

Rust batik #2
Section 2: piece 7

INSTRUCTIONS

1. Join pieces A–G as shown above right.

2. Make four paper copies *each* of foundation sections 1 and 2. Foundation piece the sections in numerical order, pressing and trimming after each piece addition.

Block center

Section 1. Make 4.

Section 2. Make 4.

3. Join a section 1 to the block center with a partial seam. Add the remaining sections in a clockwise manner. Complete the partial seam; add strips H and I. Add a section 2 to each corner.

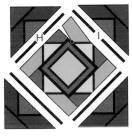

Block assembly
● = Partial seam

Cinnamon Spice

Terri Degenkolb • whimsicalquilts.com

MATERIALS

Appliqué patterns are on the enclosed disk.

△ = *Cut in half diagonally.*

⊠ = *Cut into quarters diagonally.*

Beige print #1
  1 square, 6½" x 6½" (A)

Red tone-on-tone fabric
  1 of pattern B
  1 square, 3¾" x 3¾" ⊠ (D)
  4 squares, 2⅛" x 2⅛" △ (E)
  2 squares, 2¾" x 2¾" △ (F)

Dark-brown print
  7 of pattern C
  1 square, 3¾" x 3¾" ⊠ (D)
  2 rectangles, 1½" x 10½" (G)
  2 rectangles, 1½" x 12½" (H)

Beige print #2
  2 squares, 3¾" x 3¾" ⊠ (D)
  2 squares, 2⅛" x 2⅛" △ (E)

Medium-brown tone-on-tone fabric
  2 squares, 3¾" x 3¾" ⊠ (D)
  6 squares, 2¾" x 2¾" △ (F)

INSTRUCTIONS

1. Fold A in half both ways and lightly crease to mark the center. Prepare the B and C pieces for turned-edge appliqué and blindstitch to A. Centering the appliqué, trim A to 5½" x 5½".

2. Join pieces D–H as shown to complete the block.

Block assembly and appliqué placement

Colonial Hospitality

Wendy Sheppard • ivoryspring.wordpress.com

MATERIALS

Appliqué patterns are on the enclosed disk.

△ = *Cut in half diagonally.*

Assorted beige prints
  9 squares, 4⅞" x 4⅞" △ (A)
Assorted gold prints
  36 squares, 1½" x 1½"
Assorted green
  1 *each* of patterns C–G and D–F reversed

Fusible web

INSTRUCTIONS

1. Randomly sew the beige A triangles together in pairs as shown to make the triangle squares. Sew these together to make the block background.

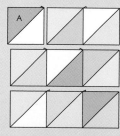

Block assembly

2. Randomly sew the gold squares together in six rows of six squares each. Sew the rows together to form a square.

3. Fold the block in half both ways and lightly crease the folds. Prepare pieces B–G for fusible appliqué, noting that B is cut from the gold-square patchwork. Use the appliqué placement diagram and the creases to position the pineapple (B) and leaves (C–G); fuse in place. Use matching thread and a blanket stitch to sew around the pieces. Use a decorative machine stitch to sew a grid through the center of the gold squares.

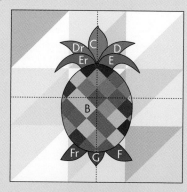

Appliqué placement

Companion Star

Marsha McCloskey • marshamccloskey.com

MATERIALS

Foundation patterns are on the enclosed disk.

◻ = Cut in half diagonally.

⊠ = Cut into quarters diagonally.

Cream toile
- 4 squares, 3½" x 3½" (A)
- 1 square, 7¼" x 7¼" ⊠ (B)

White print
- Section 1: piece 1
- Section 2: pieces 2 and 6

Black print
- Section 1: piece 2
- Section 2: pieces 1 and 7
- 1 square, 3½" x 3½" (A)

Blue print
- Section 1: pieces 3 and 4
- Section 2: pieces 3 and 5

Cream-and-blue print
- Section 2: pieces 4
- 2 squares, 3" x 3" ◻ (C)

INSTRUCTIONS

1. Make eight paper copies *each* of foundation sections 1 and 2. Foundation piece the sections in numerical order, pressing and trimming after each piece addition.

Section 1.
Make 8.

Section 2.
Make 8.

2. Join the foundation-pieced sections and pieces A–C as shown to complete the block.

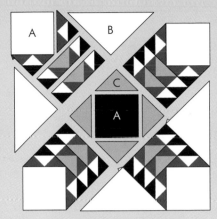

Block assembly

Croaklore

Karen Brow • javahousequilts.com

MATERIALS

Appliqué patterns are on the enclosed disk.

Gold batik
- 1 square, 7½" x 7½" (A)

Dark-green batik
- 1 *each* of patterns B, D, E, and J

Light-green print
- 1 of pattern C

Medium-green batik
- 1 of pattern F

Pink batik
- 4 rectangles, 1" x 7½" (G)

Multicolored print
- 4 rectangles, 2½" x 7½" (H)

Purple-striped fabric
- 4 squares, 3" x 3" (I)

Black Pigma Micron pen

White acrylic paint

INSTRUCTIONS

1. Prepare pieces B–F and J for turned-edge appliqué.

2. Referring to the appliqué placement diagram, pin B in place (it will be finished after the block is pieced) and appliqué pieces C–F to A in alphabetical order using a blind stitch.

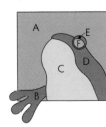

Appliqué placement

3. Pin B out of the way and assemble the block as shown.

4. Appliqué the B and J pieces in place. Use the pen and white paint to add details to the eye as shown.

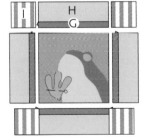

Block assembly

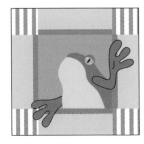

Appliqué finishing

MIXED-MEDIA

Cute as a Button

Amanda Herring • thequiltedfishpatterns.com

MATERIALS

Appliqué patterns are on the enclosed disk.

Cream tone-on-tone fabric
- 1 square, 8½" x 8½" (A)
- 2 rectangles, 2½" x 8½" (C)
- 2 rectangles, 2½" x 12½" (D)

Assorted pink and brown prints
- 32 of pattern B (16 matching sets of 2)
- 1 *each* of patterns E–G
- 1 circle, 4" diameter, for yo-yo

Buttons: 16 *each* of ⁵⁄₁₆" and ⁹⁄₁₆" diameter

Fusible web

INSTRUCTIONS

1. Prepare pieces E–G for fusible appliqué.

2. Fold A in half both ways and lightly crease the folds. Use the creases and the appliqué placement diagram to arrange and fuse the pieces on A. Use matching thread and a machine blanket stitch to secure the pieces.

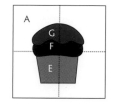

Appliqué placement

3. Layer two matching B pieces right sides together. Sew around the curve, leaving the straight edge unsewn. Clip the curved seam allowance, and then turn right side out and press. Repeat to make 16 tabs.

4. Align raw edges and space four tabs evenly along one edge of A; leave ½" at each end as shown. Lay a C piece right side down over the tabs and sew in place.

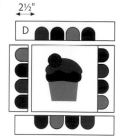

5. Repeat on the opposite side of A. Press the seam allowances toward A. Repeat the process at the top and bottom of the block with tabs and D pieces.

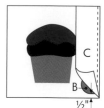

6. Stack a large and small button and sew to each tab as shown in the block photo. Referring to "Yo-Yos" on page 125, make a yo-yo and sew it to the cupcake.

Block assembly

Daisez

Dodi Lee Paulsen • twosashquilts.com

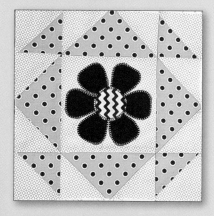

MATERIALS

Appliqué patterns are on the enclosed disk.

◻ = *Cut in half diagonally.*
⊠ = *Cut into quarters diagonally.*

Light-blue print
- 1 square, 7½" x 7½" (A)
- 4 squares, 3⅞" x 3⅞" ◻ (E)
- 2 squares, 3⅞" x 3⅞" (F)

Red solid
- 6 of pattern B

White-and-red striped fabric
- 1 of pattern C

Blue dotted fabric
- 1 square, 7¼" x 7¼" ⊠ (D)
- 2 squares, 3⅞" x 3⅞" (F)

Fusible web

INSTRUCTIONS

1. Referring to "Triangle Squares" on page 124, use the blue-print and dotted F squares to make four units.

Make 4.

2. Prepare the B and C pieces for fusible appliqué; fuse to A as shown. Using a machine blanket stitch and contrasting thread, stitch around the flower pieces. Centering the flower, trim A to 6½" x 6½".

3. Sew the pieces together as shown to complete the block.

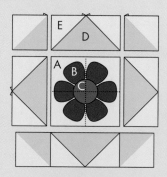

Block assembly and appliqué placement

MIXED-MEDIA

Dot Goes to School

Jane Quinn • quiltinginthecountry.com

MATERIALS

Embroidery pattern is on the enclosed disk.

White tone-on-tone fabric
2 rectangles, 7½" x 8¼" (A)

Assorted red, green, yellow, and black prints
1 rectangle, 3¾" x 7¼" (B)
1 rectangle, 2½" x 9¾" (C)
1 rectangle, 3¼" x 9¾" (D)
1 rectangle, 3¾" x 4½" (E)
1 rectangle, 3¾" x 8½" (F)

Brown Pigma Micron pen .01
Embroidery floss: Black
Crayons
Paper towel

INSTRUCTIONS

1. Fold one A piece in half both ways and lightly crease the folds. Using the creases as a guide for placement, trace the embroidery design onto the fabric with the pen.

Embroidery placement

2. Use the crayons to color in the design. Place a paper towel over the design and set the crayon color with a hot, dry iron.

3. Layer the marked A piece on top of the plain A piece and baste them together. Use a backstitch (page 126) to embroider the design through both layers. Use a satin stitch (page 126) in the flower. Remove the basting stitches. Centering the design, trim to 6½" x 7¼".

4. Join pieces B–F to the center square as shown to complete the block.

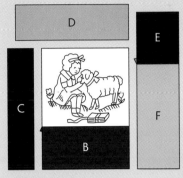

Block assembly

Egg Plant

Susan Geddes • quiltersnewsletter.com

MATERIALS

Appliqué pattern is on the enclosed disk.

◻ = *Cut in half diagonally.*
⊠ = *Cut into quarters diagonally.*

Gray print
4 squares, 2⅝" x 2⅝" (A)

Purple tone-on-tone fabric
2 squares, 2⅝" x 2⅝" (A)
1 square, 4¼" x 4¼" ⊠ (B)

Tan print
1 square, 6⅞" x 6⅞" ◻ (C)
1 rectangle, 6½" x 12½" (D)

Assorted prints
14 of pattern E

Rickrack: Black
12" length of black cut into 3 pieces: one 5" and two 3½"

Fusible web
Buttons: 1" diameter, 3 each

INSTRUCTIONS

1. Join pieces A–C as shown to make the bottom section of the block. On D, mark the center as shown by the dotted line; measure 3¾" from the center on both sides and mark for stem placement.

2. Placing rickrack at the marks, sew the rickrack stems to D with matching thread and a straight stitch. Prepare the E pieces for fusible appliqué. Arrange them on D as shown and fuse in place.

3. Sew the upper and lower sections together, catching the rickrack ends in the seam. Sew a button at the top of each rickrack stem.

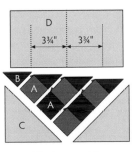

Block assembly

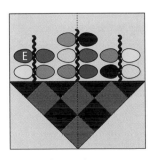

Appliqué placement

Eventide Bloom

Jacquelynne Steves • thenoblewife.com

MATERIALS

Appliqué patterns are on the enclosed disk.

◻ = *Cut in half diagonally.*

Brown pindot fabric
1 square, 10" x 10" (A)

Assorted pastel prints and solids
1 *each* of patterns B–D, F–N
2 *each* of pattern E

Pastel-green print
2 squares, 6⅞" x 6⅞" ◻ (L)

INSTRUCTIONS

1. Prepare pieces B–N for fusible appliqué.

2. Fold A into quarters diagonally and lightly crease. Referring to the diagram, use the creases as guidelines to position and fuse the appliqués. Use matching thread and a zigzag stitch to sew the pieces in place. Centering the appliqué, trim A to 9" x 9".

3. Sew the L triangles to A as shown to complete the block.

Block assembly and appliqué placement

Evergreen

Patty Heath • quiltersnewsletter.com

MATERIALS

Appliqué patterns are on the enclosed disk.

◻ = *Cut in half diagonally.*

Medium-green tone-on-tone fabric
2 squares, 3⅞" x 3⅞" (A)
1 of pattern F

Dark-green print
2 squares, 3⅞" x 3⅞" (A)

Medium-purple tone-on-tone fabric
6 squares, 3" x 3" ◻ (B)

Cream print
2 squares, 3" x 3" ◻ (B)

Cream-and-green print
4 squares, 3⅞" x 3⅞" ◻ (C)

Multicolored print
1 square, 6½" x 6½" (D)

Black-on-white print
4 of pattern E

Light-purple tone-on-tone fabric
1 of pattern G

Fusible web

INSTRUCTIONS

1. Referring to "Triangle Squares" on page 124, use the medium-green and dark-green A squares to make four units.

2. Assemble the triangle squares and pieces B–D as shown in the block assembly diagram above right. Fold the block into quarters diagonally and lightly crease the folds.

3. Prepare pieces E–G for fusible appliqué. Note that the circle in the center of the G piece is cut out.

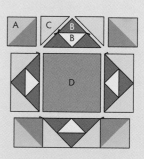

Block assembly

4. Referring to the appliqué placement diagram and using the creased folds as a guide, position and fuse the pieces to the block in alphabetical order. Use matching thread and a straight machine stitch to secure the appliqués.

Appliqué placement

Flip Side

Sara Tuttle Khammash

MATERIALS

Appliqué patterns are on the enclosed disk.

Green tone-on-tone fabric
- 2 squares, 6½" x 6½" (A)
- 2 squares, 3" x 3" (B)
- 2 *each* of patterns C reversed and D reversed
- 1 of pattern E

Yellow tone-on-tone fabric
- 2 squares, 6½" x 6½" (A)
- 2 squares, 3" x 3" (B)
- 2 *each* of patterns C and D

Fusible web

INSTRUCTIONS

1. Referring to "Stitch and Flip" on page 124, join the A and B squares as shown.

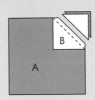

Make 2 of each.

2. Prepare pieces C–E for fusible appliqué. Fuse the C–D reversed pieces as shown above right. With matching thread, blanket-stitch the edges of the appliqués.

Make 2 of each.

3. Join the appliquéd sections as shown. Fuse the E circle to the block center and blanket-stitch the edges with matching thread.

Block assembly

Flower Frenzy

Cheryl Brown • quilterchic.com

MATERIALS

Appliqué pattern is on the enclosed disk.

◻ = *Cut in half diagonally.*

Purple batik and green-dotted batik
- 1 square, 9⅞" x 9⅞", from *each* fabric ◻ (A) (You'll have 1 extra triangle from each fabric.)
- 1 of pattern B from *each* fabric
- 9 squares, 2⅞" x 2⅞", from *each* fabric (C)
- 1 square, 2½" x 2½", from *each* fabric (D)

INSTRUCTIONS

1. Referring to "Triangle Squares" on page 124, pair the purple and green C squares to make 18 units.

Make 18.

2. Prepare the B pieces for turned-edge appliqué. Mark the center of the A triangles by folding in half diagonally and creasing. Matching the fold lines of the A and B pieces as shown, appliqué the pieces in place with a blind stitch.

3. Sew the appliquéd triangles together. Centering the appliqué, trim the square to 8½" x 8½". Using the triangle squares and D squares, assemble the block as shown.

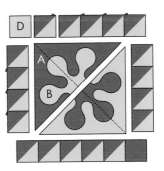

Block assembly and appliqué placement

Flowers for Ewe

Paula Stoddard • pacificpatchwork.com

MATERIALS

Appliqué and embroidery patterns are on the enclosed disk.

4 assorted green prints
  1 square, 3½" x 3½", from *each* fabric (A)
Tan dotted fabric
  1 rectangle, 9½" x 12½" (B)
Black tone-on-tone fabric
  4 of pattern C
  1 of pattern E
  3 of pattern F

Cream tone-on-tone fabric
  1 of pattern D
Purple tone-on-tone and pink tone-on-tone fabrics
  5 of pattern G, from *each* fabric
Gold tone-on-tone fabric
  2 of pattern H
Green-dotted fabric
  4 of pattern I
Fusible web
Embroidery floss: Colors to match appliqués

INSTRUCTIONS

1. Join the four A squares and sew to B as shown. Fold the block in half both ways and lightly crease the folds.

2. Prepare pieces C–I for fusible appliqué. Use the creases and the appliqué placement diagram as a guide to arrange the appliqués on the block; fuse in place. Use matching embroidery floss and a hand blanket stitch (page 126) to sew around the pieces. Use

green floss and a chain stitch (page 126) to embroider the flower stems.

Block assembly

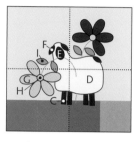

Appliqué and embroidery placement

Friends

Lynette Anderson-O'Rourke • lynetteandersondesigns.typepad.com

MATERIALS

Appliqué and embroidery patterns are on the enclosed disk.

Cream tone-on-tone fabric
  1 square, 8½" x 8½" (A)
Green tone-on-tone fabric
  1 of pattern B
Brown tone-on-tone fabric
  1 *each* of patterns C–F

Brown print
  1 *each* of patterns G and H
Dark-red print
  4 rectangles, 2½" x 8½" (I)
Cream print
  4 squares, 2½" x 2½" (J)
Embroidery floss: Green, brown, cream, and black

INSTRUCTIONS

1. Prepare pieces B–H for turned-edge appliqué. Referring to the diagram for placement, use matching thread and a blind stitch to appliqué the pieces in alphabetical order to A.

2. Referring to "Embroidery Stitches" on page 126, use a lazy daisy stitch and French knots to add sprigs of grass to B. Use a backstitch and satin stitch to embroider features on the cat and a running stitch to outline B, G, and H. Embroider the bird using a backstitch and a French knot for the eye.

3. Join pieces I and J to A as shown to complete the block.

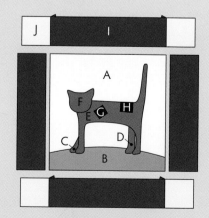

Block assembly and appliqué placement

Full Bloom

Bonnie Sullivan • allthroughthenight.net

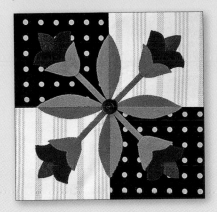

MATERIALS

Appliqué patterns are on the enclosed disk.

Cream-striped flannel
2 squares, 6½" x 6½" (A)
Black dotted flannel
2 squares, 6½" x 6½" (A)
Medium-green and dark-green wool
4 of pattern B from *each* fabric
1 of pattern C from *each* fabric
2 of pattern F from *each* fabric

Light-red wool
4 of pattern D
Dark-red wool
4 of pattern E
Button: Black, 1" diameter

INSTRUCTIONS

1. Sew the A squares together as shown.

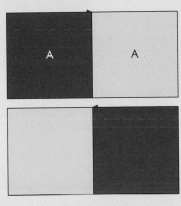

Block assembly

2. Refer to the appliqué placement diagram to arrange pieces B–F; baste or pin in place. Using matching thread and a whipstitch (page 123), sew the appliqués in place. Sew the button to the center as shown in the photo.

Appliqué placement

Garden Flight

Kathy Schmitz • kathyschmitz.com

MATERIALS

Embroidery pattern is on the enclosed disk.

◻ = Cut in half diagonally.

Green tone-on-tone fabric
2 squares, 3½" x 3½" ◻ (A)
2 strips, ¾" x 8" (C)
2 strips, ¾" x 8½" (D)
4 squares, 2½" x 2½" (G)

Red tone-on-tone fabric
2 squares, 3½" x 3½" ◻ (A)
8 squares, 3¼" x 3¼" (E)
Beige tone-on-tone fabric
2 squares, 4⅝" x 4⅝" ◻ (B)
32 squares, 1⅞" x 1⅞" (F)
Embroidery floss: Red
Freezer paper

INSTRUCTIONS

1. Referring to "Fast Flying Geese" on page 124, use the red E and beige F squares to make 32 flying-geese units.

Make 32.

2. Sew pieces A–D and G together with the flying geese to complete the block.

3. Trace the embroidery pattern onto freezer paper and iron onto the wrong side of the B triangles using the seam

line as a guide. Using a light box, trace the design onto each B triangle. Use an outline stitch (page 126) and two strands of floss to embroider each design, filling in the circles with a satin stitch (page 126).

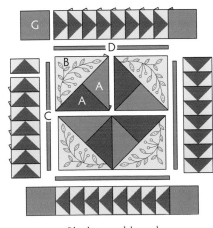

Block assembly and embroidery placement

The Gilded Age

Meg Hawkey • crabapplehillstudio.com

MATERIALS

Embroidery pattern is on the enclosed disk.

Cream tone-on-tone fabric
1 square, 15" x 15" (A)

Natural muslin
1 square, 15" x 15" (A)

Embroidery floss: Assorted shades of gold and brown

Brown Micron Pigma pen, .01

INSTRUCTIONS

1. Fold the cream square in half both ways and lightly crease the folds. Using the creases as a placement guide, trace the embroidery design onto the fabric with the pen. Layer the cream square on top of the muslin square and baste them together.

2. Referring to "Embroidery Stitches" on page 126, use a blanket stitch and various shades of gold and brown to stitch the flowers through both fabric layers. Make French knots with dark-brown floss for the flower centers. Use a lazy daisy stitch and greenish-gold floss for the leaves. Make cross-stitches on the urn with gold floss and on the border with dark-brown floss. Use a backstitch or stem stitch for the remainder of the stitching.

3. After the embroidery is complete, remove the basting stitches and press the block. Centering the design, trim the block to 12½" x 12½". If you don't have a 12½" square ruler, you can cut a piece of freezer paper to that size and use it as a template to center the stitching.

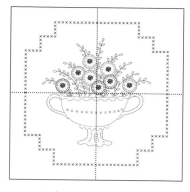

Embroidery placement

Holiday Tea

Melissa Harris and Arlene Stamper • quiltcompany.com

MATERIALS

Appliqué patterns are on the enclosed disk.

Red print
1 rectangle, 5½" x 6" (A)
1 rectangle, 2½" x 4" (E)

Cream tone-on-tone fabric
4 squares, 1½" x 1½" (B)
2 rectangles, 3½" x 4¾" (F)
2 rectangles, 3¾" x 4" (G)
1 rectangle, 2½" x 12½" (I)

Tan floral print
2 squares, 2" x 2" (C)
2 rectangles, 2" x 3¾" (H)
1 rectangle, 2½" x 12½" (I)

Green tone-on-tone fabric
1 rectangle, 1½" x 4" (D)
1 of pattern L

Red polka-dot fabric
1 *each* of patterns J and K

Fusible web

INSTRUCTIONS

1. Referring to "Stitch and Flip" on page 124 and noting the orientation of A, sew the cream B and tan floral C squares to A to make unit 1. Sew the cream B squares to the green D piece to make unit 2.

Unit 1.
Make 1.

Unit 2.
Make 1.

2. Join units 1 and 2 with pieces E–I as shown to make the block.

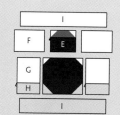

Block assembly

3. Prepare pieces J–L for fusible appliqué. Referring to the appliqué placement diagram, arrange the appliqués on the block. Use matching thread and a machine blanket stitch (page 126) to secure the appliqués.

Appliqué placement

MIXED-MEDIA

How About a Hug?

Heidi Pridemore • thewhimsicalworkshop.com

MATERIALS

Appliqué patterns are on the enclosed disk.

Purple tone-on-tone fabric
  1 square, 8½" x 8½" (A)
Green print
  2 rectangles, 2½" x 8½" (B)
  2 rectangles, 2½" x 12½" (C)
Brown solid
  1 *each* of patterns D, F, I, and J

Pink tone-on-tone fabric
  1 *each* of patterns E and G
Gold tone-on-tone fabric
  1 *each* of patterns H and M
White solid
  2 of pattern K
Black solid
  2 of pattern L
  1 of pattern N
Fusible web
Stabilizer
Embroidery floss: Black

INSTRUCTIONS

1. Join pieces A–C as shown.

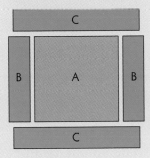

Block assembly

2. Prepare pieces D–N for fusible appliqué.

3. Fold the block in half both ways and lightly crease. Use the creases and the appliqué placement diagram as guides to arrange pieces D–N on the block. Fuse them in alphabetical order.

4. With stabilizer underneath, use brown thread and a machine blanket stitch to sew around all pieces except K (use white thread) and L and N (use black thread). Use black floss and a backstitch (page 126) to hand embroider the mouth.

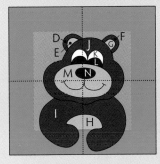

Appliqué placement

Hugs and Kisses

Linda Lum DeBono • lindalumdebono.com

MATERIALS

Appliqué pattern is on the enclosed disk.

Cream print #1 and black print #1
  2 squares, 4⅞" x 4⅞", from *each* fabric (A)
Pink print and green print
  2 squares, 4½" x 4½", from *each* fabric (B)
Cream print #2
  1 square, 4½" x 4½" (B)

Teal print
  6 of pattern C
Black print #2
  1 circle, 4½"-diameter, for yo-yo
Fusible web

INSTRUCTIONS

1. Referring to "Triangle Squares" on page 124, use the cream #1 and black #1 A squares to make 4 units.

2. Join the units and B squares as shown to make the block.

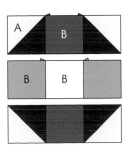

Block assembly

3. Prepare the C pieces for fusible appliqué. Arrange them on the block as shown and fuse in place. Use matching thread and a machine blanket stitch to secure the petals.

4. Referring to "Yo-Yos" on page 125, make a yo-yo from the black circle. Sew the yo-yo to the center of the block.

Appliqué placement

Irish Spring Surprise

Peg Spradlin • handicraftsbypeg.com

MATERIALS

Appliqué patterns are on the enclosed disk.

Green tone-on-tone fabric
12 squares, 1½" x 1½" (A)

Aqua print
12 squares, 1½" x 1½" (A)
8 squares, 2½" x 2½" (B)
4 rectangles, 2½" x 4½" (C)
1 square, 4½" x 4½" (D)

White tone-on-tone fabric
16 squares, 1½" x 1½" (A)
6 of pattern F

Medium-teal print
16 squares, 1½" x 1½" (A)

Dark-teal print
8 squares, 1½" x 1½" (A)

Yellow tone-on-tone fabric
1 of pattern E

Monofilament

INSTRUCTIONS

1. Join pieces A–D as shown to piece the block.

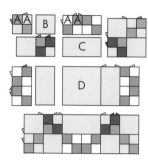

Block assembly

2. Prepare the E and F pieces for turned-edge appliqué.

3. Fold the block in half both ways and lightly crease. Use the creases and the appliqué placement diagram as guides to arrange the appliqués on the block. Use monofilament and a machine blind stitch to appliqué the pieces in place.

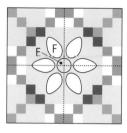

Appliqué placement

Maywood Blossom

Deborah Johnson • inthedoghousedesigns.com

MATERIALS

Appliqué patterns are on the enclosed disk.

Cream tone-on-tone fabric
1 square, 8½" x 8½" (A)
4 rectangles, 1½" x 8½" (B)

Blue print
4 rectangles, 1½" x 8½" (B)
4 squares, 2½" x 2½" (C)

Red tone-on-tone fabric
2 *each* of patterns D and D reversed
1 of pattern E

Green tone-on-tone fabric
1 *each* of patterns F, G, G reversed, and H

Fusible web

INSTRUCTIONS

1. Join pieces A–C as shown to piece the block.

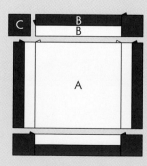

Block assembly

2. Prepare pieces D–H for fusible appliqué.

3. Fold the block in half both ways and lightly crease. Use the creases and the appliqué placement diagram as guides to arrange the appliqués on the block. Fuse them in place.

4. Use matching thread and a machine satin stitch to sew around the appliqués.

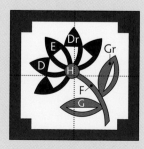

Appliqué placement

No Ordinary Flake

Susan Marth • suznquilts.com

MATERIALS

Appliqué patterns are on the enclosed disk.

Medium-brown and dark-brown prints

  2 squares, 6½" x 6½", from *each* fabric (A)

Light-pink print
  6 of pattern B

Dark-pink print
  6 of pattern C
  1 of pattern D

Fusible web

INSTRUCTIONS

1. Join the four A squares as shown.

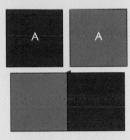

Block assembly

2. Prepare pieces B–D for fusible appliqué. Use the seam lines and the appliqué placement diagram as guides to arrange the appliqués on the block. Fuse in alphabetical order.

3. Use black thread and a machine blanket stitch to sew around the appliqués.

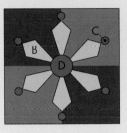

Appliqué placement

Pocket Full of Posies

Laura West Kong • laurawestkong.com

MATERIALS

Appliqué patterns are on the enclosed disk.

Green-and-pink print #1
  Foundation piece 1
Black-on-white print
  Foundation pieces 2 and 3
  1 rectangle, 7¾" x 12½" (A)
  2 rectangles, 4" x 5¼" (B)
Green-and-pink print #2
  1 rectangle, 1½" x 5½" (C)

Dark-green solid
  1 bias strip, 1¼" x 8", for stems
Pink solid
  15 of pattern D
Yellow print
  Scraps for covered buttons
Fusible web
Buttons: 3 to cover, 1¼" diameter; 1 green, ⅝" diameter

INSTRUCTIONS

1. Foundation piece the flower pocket in numerical order, pressing and trimming after each piece addition.

2. Refer to "Bias Strips" on page 122 to make a stem; cut the stem into three

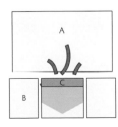

Block assembly

pieces. Referring to the block assembly diagram, pin the stems to A. Assemble the block as shown.

3. Prepare the D petals for fusible appliqué. Fuse the petals to the block as shown. Using matching thread and a small zigzag stitch, stitch around the flowers and stems.

Appliqué placement

4. Follow the manufacturer's instructions to cover the buttons. Sew the covered buttons to the flower centers and the small button to the pocket.

MIXED-MEDIA

Pouncer

Sue Marsh • wpcreek.com

MATERIALS

Appliqué patterns are on the enclosed disk.

Black tone-on-tone fabric
1 rectangle, 5½" x 9½" (A)
1 of pattern N

Black-on-white print #1
2 rectangles, 1" x 5½" (B)
2 rectangles, 1" x 10½" (C)

Black-on-white print #2
1 rectangle, 2½" x 10½" (D)
1 rectangle, 2½" x 8½" (E)

Black-on-white print #3
1 square, 4" x 4" (F)

Black-on-white print #4
1 *each* of patterns H, I, K, K reversed, L, Q, and Q reversed

Black-on-white print #5
1 *each* of patterns O and O reversed

Pink tone-on-tone fabric
2 squares, 4" x 4" (F)
1 *each* of patterns J, J reversed, M, and P

White-on-black print
1 rectangle, 4½" x 12½" (G)

Fusible web

INSTRUCTIONS

1. Fold an F square in half diagonally, wrong sides together. Fold in half again. Repeat with the remaining F squares to make three prairie points.

2. Pin or baste the prairie points to G as shown. Then assemble pieces A–E and G as shown.

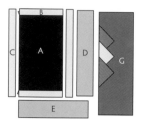

Block assembly

3. Prepare pieces H–P reversed for fusible appliqué. Fuse the appliqués to the block in alphabetical order as shown. Using black thread, satin stitch around the appliqués. Satin stitch the eyebrows and make French knots (page 126) for the eyes.

Appliqué placement

Queen of Hearts

Vicki Bellino • bloomcreek.com

MATERIALS

Appliqué patterns are on the enclosed disk.

Assorted white prints
4 squares, 5½" x 5½" (A)
4 of pattern H
7 rectangles, 1½" x 3" (J)
2 rectangles, 1½" x 2¾" (K)

Assorted red prints
4 *each* of patterns B, F, and G
1 *each* of patterns C and D
2 *each* of patterns E and E reversed
12 of pattern I
7 rectangles, 1½" x 3" (J)
2 rectangles, 1½" x 2¾" (K)

Fusible web

INSTRUCTIONS

1. Join the four A squares as shown.

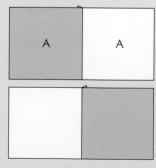

Block assembly

2. Prepare pieces B–I for fusible appliqué. Referring to the diagram and using the seams as a guide, position and fuse the appliqués to the block in alphabetical order. Use matching thread to machine blanket-stitch around the appliqués.

3. Add the J and K pieces as shown to complete the block.

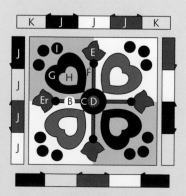

Appliqué placement
and block assembly

Rose Trellis

Elizabeth Scott • latebloomerquilts.com

MATERIALS

Appliqué patterns are on the enclosed disk.

Cream-and-green print
   2 squares, 3⅞" x 3⅞" (A)
Light-green print #1
   2 squares, 3⅞" x 3⅞" (A)
   4 squares, 3½" x 3½" (C)
Cream dotted print
   12 rectangles, 2" x 3½" (B)
Light-green print #2
   1 square, 3½" x 3½" (C)

Yellow print
   4 squares, 2" x 2" (D)
Assorted green, red, peach, and cream prints
   5 of pattern E
   3 of pattern F
   3 of pattern G
Fusible web

INSTRUCTIONS

1. Referring to "Triangle Squares" on page 124, pair the cream A and green A squares to make four triangle squares.

2. Join the triangle squares and pieces B–D as shown to make the block.

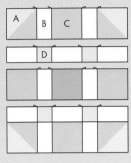

Block assembly

3. Prepare pieces E–G for fusible appliqué. Referring to the diagram for placement, fuse the appliqués to the block in alphabetical order. Using matching thread, machine blanket-stitch (page 126) around the appliqués.

Appliqué placement

Sew Little Time

Jina Barney • jinabarneydesignz.com

MATERIALS

Appliqué patterns are on the enclosed disk.

Aqua tone-on-tone fabric
   1 square, 10½" x 10½" (A)
   2 rectangles, 1" x 11½" (F)
   2 rectangles, 1" x 12½" (G)
Assorted prints and tone-on-tone fabrics
   1 square, 1⅞" x 1⅞" (B)
   3 rectangles, 1⅛" x 3¼" (C)
   1 rectangle, 1¼" x 4" (D)
   40 squares, 1½" x 1½" (E)
   1 set of appliqué pieces
Buttons: 3, each ½" diameter
Embroidery floss: Pink

INSTRUCTIONS

1. Sew pieces B–D together as shown to make the "quilt block." Trim the ends of C and D even with B as shown. Prepare the quilt block and other appliqués for turned-edge appliqué.

"Quilt block" assembly

2. Fold A in half both ways and lightly crease. Use the creases and the appliqué placement diagram as guides to arrange the appliqués on A, tucking the long edge of the quilt block under the sewing-machine bed. Use matching thread and a blind stitch (page 126) to secure the appliqués. Use the floss and a backstitch to stitch the "thread"

on the sewing machine as shown on the appliqué pattern. Centering the appliqué, trim the block to 9½" x 9½".

3. Randomly sew together two sets of nine E squares; join each to one side of A as shown. Randomly join two sets of 11 E squares and sew them to the top and bottom of A. Add the F and G strips as shown. Sew buttons to the sewing machine as shown in the photo to complete the block.

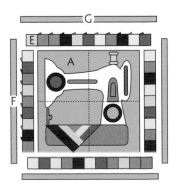

Appliqué placement and block assembly

Simple Celebration

Anita Grossman Solomon • makeitsimpler.com

MATERIALS

Foundation pattern is on the enclosed disk.

⬜ = *Cut in half diagonally.*

Cream print
Pieces 1, 4, and 5
Dark-gray print, dark-pink print, black print #1, and black print #2
Pieces 2 and 3 from *each* fabric

Gray-and-pink print
1 square, 4⅛" x 4⅛" (A)
Olive-green tone-on-tone fabric
2 squares, 3½" x 3½" ⬜ (B)
4 squares, 2⅞" x 2⅞" (C)
Black tone-on-tone fabric
2 squares, 4½" x 4½" ⬜ (D)

INSTRUCTIONS

1. Make four paper copies of the foundation pattern.

2. Foundation piece each pattern in numerical order, pressing and trimming after each piece addition. **Note:** Notice that the fabric used in piece 3 in one section will be used in piece 2 in the next section.

3. Join pieces A–D with the foundation-pieced units as shown to complete the block.

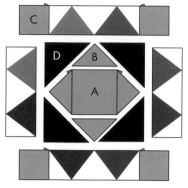

Block assembly

Sparkles Snow Globe

Mary Jane Carey • oldstnick.net

MATERIALS

Appliqué patterns are on the enclosed disk.

White-and-blue print
1 square, 9½" x 9½" (A)
Blue dotted fabric
1 of pattern B
Brown tone-on-tone fabric
1 of pattern C
Light-green tone-on-tone fabric
1 *each* of patterns D–F
10 squares, 2½" x 2½" (H)

Green print
1 of pattern G
White-on-white print
10 squares, 2½" x 2½" (H)
Red tone-on-tone fabric
4 strips, 1" x 8½" (I)
Baby rickrack: 8" length of white
10 iron-on crystals

INSTRUCTIONS

1. Prepare pieces B–G for turned-edge appliqué.

2. Fold A in half both ways and lightly crease. Use the creases and the diagram as guides to arrange the appliqués on A. Add the rickrack to D–F as shown, tucking the ends under the pieces. Using a blind stitch, hand sew the pieces in place. Centering the appliqué, trim the block to 8½" x 8½".

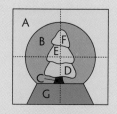

Appliqué placement

3. Fold the red I strips in half lengthwise with the wrong sides together and press. Matching the raw edges, lay an I strip along one edge of A; machine baste ⅛" from the raw edge. Repeat to baste an I to each side of A. Join the H squares as shown and sew to the outer edges of the block.

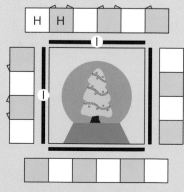

Block assembly

4. Add crystals to the tree as desired.

Spring on the Square

Cori Blunt • chitterchatterdesigns.com

MATERIALS

Appliqué patterns are on the enclosed disk.

White tone-on-tone fabric
- 1 square, 8½" x 8½" (A)
- 4 of pattern C
- 2 rectangles, 2½" x 8½" (D)
- 2 rectangles, 2½" x 12½" (E)

Mottled-green solid
- 4 of pattern B
- 16 of pattern G

Blue tone-on-tone fabric
- 1 of pattern F

Medium-blue solid
- 4 of pattern H

Light-blue solid
- 4 of pattern I

Embroidery floss: Green

INSTRUCTIONS

1. Prepare pieces B, C, and F–I for turned-edge appliqué. The long straight edges of C don't need to be turned under.

2. Fold A in half both ways and lightly crease. Use the creases as a guide to arrange the appliqués. Use matching thread and a blind stitch to appliqué the B arcs in place, followed by the C pieces. Trim away the A fabric from behind each C, ¼" outside the appliqué seam line.

3. Join the D and E pieces to the block as shown above right.

4. Appliqué the remaining pieces in alphabetical order. Using a stem stitch, embroider the stems as indicated in red.

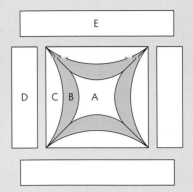

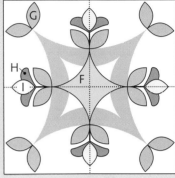

Appliqué placement

Summer Garden

Karla Eisenach • sweetwaterscrapbook.com

MATERIALS

Appliqué patterns are on the enclosed disk.

4 assorted light-cream-and-black prints
- 1 square, 6½" x 6½", from *each* fabric (A)

Pale-green print
- 1 of pattern B

Cream-and-black polka-dot print
- 1 of pattern C

Fusible web

Embroidery floss: Black

INSTRUCTIONS

1. Sew the four A squares together as shown.

2. Prepare pieces B and C for fusible appliqué (the pieces will need to be flipped to trace the whole pattern). Fold B and C into quarters and gently crease. Align the folds with the block seam lines and fuse the pieces to the pieced block.

3. Using black floss, hand blanket-stitch (page 126) around all edges of B and C.

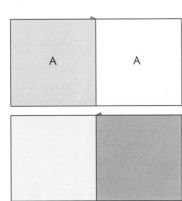

Block assembly

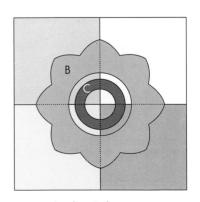

Appliqué placement

Summer's Best

Ann Weber • ginghamgirls.biz

MATERIALS

Appliqué patterns are on the enclosed disk.

◻ = *Cut in half diagonally.*

⊠ = *Cut into quarters diagonally.*

Yellow tone-on-tone fabric
4 squares, 4¾" x 4¾" (A)

Cream tone-on-tone fabric
1 square, 4¾" x 4¾" (A)
1 square, 7¼" x 7¼" ⊠ (B)
2 squares, 3⅞" x 3⅞" ◻ (C)

Green print
1 bias strip, 1⅜" x 31"

Assorted pink and green prints for flowers and leaves
11 of pattern D
10 of pattern E
2 *each* of patterns F and G

Fusible web

INSTRUCTIONS

1. Sew pieces A–C together as shown to make the block.

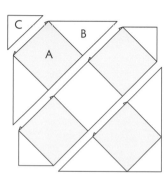

Block assembly

2. Referring to "Bias Strips" on page 122, make a bias strip. Position it as shown. Using a straight stitch, sew close to both edges of the strip.

3. Prepare pieces D–G for fusible appliqué; fuse the flowers and leaves as shown. Use a blanket stitch and matching thread to stitch around all of the appliqués.

Appliqué placement

Sunday Best

Rosalie Quinlan • rosaliequinlandesigns.typepad.com

MATERIALS

Appliqué patterns are on the enclosed disk.

Pink print
1 square, 11½" x 11½" (A)

Medium-green dotted fabric
1 of pattern B
4 of pattern D
8 of pattern G

Pale-green dotted fabric
1 of pattern C

Pink dotted fabric
1 of pattern E

Blue-checked fabric
4 of pattern F
2 rectangles, 1½" x 10½" (I)
2 rectangles, 1½" x 12½" (J)

Red-checked fabric
4 of pattern H

INSTRUCTIONS

1. Prepare pieces B–H for turned-edge appliqué.

2. Fold A in half both ways and lightly crease. Use the creases and the diagram as guides to arrange the appliqués on A. Use matching thread and a blind stitch to hand stitch the pieces in place. Centering the appliqué, trim the block to 10½" x 10½".

3. Add the I and J strips to A to complete the block.

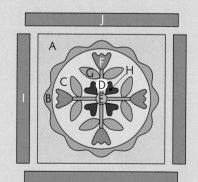

Appliqué placement and block assembly

Sunny Day

Vicki Lynn Oehlke • willowberry-lane.com

MATERIALS

Appliqué patterns are on the enclosed disk.

◻ = *Cut in half diagonally.*

Off-white tone-on-tone fabric
1 square, 6" x 6" (A)

Green tone-on-tone fabric
10 of pattern B
4 squares, 2⅞" x 2⅞" (F)

Yellow print
10 of pattern C

Blue print #1
1 circle, 4"-diameter, for yo-yo

Blue print #2
2 rectangles, 2" x 6" (D)
2 rectangles, 2" x 9" (E)

Off-white print
4 squares, 2⅞" x 2⅞" (F)
6 squares, 2⅞" x 2⅞" ◻ (H)

Yellow dotted print
4 squares, 2½" x 2½" (G)

Button: ½" diameter

INSTRUCTIONS

1. With right sides together, sew the B leaves together in pairs, leaving an opening between the dots and backstitching. Turn the leaves right sides out and press. Make five. Using the same method, make five C flower petals. Baste across the raw edges of the petals with a long running stitch. Pull the basting thread to gather the edges.

2. Referring to "Yo-Yos" on page 125, use the blue print #1 circle to make a yo-yo.

3. Arrange the leaves, petals, and yo-yo on A and tack in place to form a flower shape. Add a button to the middle of the yo-yo.

4. Referring to "Triangle Squares" on page 124, use the green and off-white F squares to make eight units. Join the D, E, G, and H pieces and the triangle squares as shown to complete the block.

Appliqué placement
and block assembly

Sweet Dreams

Tricia Cribbs • friendfolks.com

MATERALS

Embroidery pattern is on the enclosed disk.

Cream tone-on-tone fabric
1 square, 9½" x 9½" (A)

Natural muslin
1 square, 9½" x 9½" (A)

Dark-pink striped fabric
4 rectangles, 1" x 8½" (B)

Cream print
4 rectangles, 2" x 8½" (C)

Pink print
4 squares, 2½" x 2½" (D)

Brown Pigma Micron pen, .01
Embroidery floss: Red

INSTRUCTIONS

1. Fold the cream A square in half both ways and lightly crease. Using the creases as a guide, trace the embroidery design onto the cream fabric with the pen. Layer the cream fabric right side up on top of the muslin square and baste together.

2. Hand embroider through both layers using a stem stitch and French knots (page 126). Use a satin stitch for the lips and buttons. After the embroidery is complete, remove the basting stitches. Centering the design, trim the block to 8½" x 8½".

3. Join pieces B–D to A as shown to complete the block.

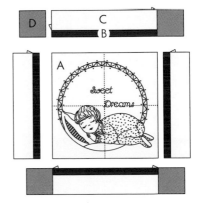

Embroidery placement
and block assembly

Thoughtful Star

Janet Bate

MATERIALS

Embroidery pattern is on the enclosed disk.

⬜ = *Cut in half diagonally.*

Cream solid
   1 square, 6" x 6"

Tan-and-cream multicolored print
   4 squares, 4½" x 4½" (A)
Black print
   4 squares, 3⅜" x 3⅜" (B)
Cream dotted and black-and-tan prints
   4 squares, 2⅞" x 2⅞", from *each* fabric ⬜ (C)
Fine-point removable marker
Embroidery floss: Tan and black

INSTRUCTIONS

1. Iron a piece of freezer paper to the wrong side of the 6" cream square. Using the removable marker, draw a 4" x 4" square on the cream fabric. Trace the key and the quotation within the square as shown.

2. Backstitch (page 126) using two strands of tan floss for the key and one strand of black floss for the quotation. Trim the embroidered piece to 4½" x 4½".

3. Sew pieces A–C together as shown to complete the block.

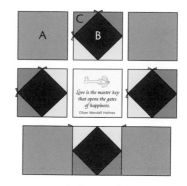

Block assembly

Wool Crazy Crow

JoAnn Mullaly • cloft.com

MATERIALS

Patchwork and appliqué patterns are on the enclosed disk.

Assorted red, gold, green, and black wool scraps
   1 *each* of patterns A–F and I–P
   5 of pattern Q
Green plaid wool
   2 rectangles, 2½" x 8½" (G)
   2 rectangles, 2½" x 12½" (H)

Muslin or osnaburg
   1 square, 8½" x 8½"
Batting
   1 square, 12½" x 12½"
Pearl cotton: Size 8, in colors to match wool
#2 crewel needles

INSTRUCTIONS

1. Position pieces A–F right sides up on top of the muslin or osnaburg square, slightly overlapping the piece edges. Pin or baste in place. Using a ¼" seam allowance, sew G pieces to the top and bottom of the block as shown. Repeat to add an H piece to each side.

2. Layer the block and batting. Referring to "Embroidery Stitches" on page 126, embroider the pieces as shown on the pattern, stitching through the batting to secure.

3. Using matching thread and a hand blanket stitch (page 126), add pieces I–P in alphabetical order, sewing around each piece. Add the Q pieces, embroidering each one with matching thread as shown on the pattern.

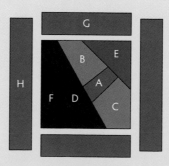

Block assembly

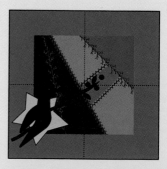

Embroidery and appliqué placement

Settings and Yardages for 12" Blocks

Use these sample settings as a guide to joining multiple 12" x 12" blocks into lap- and bed-sized quilts. Before cutting and sewing, measure the length and width of your mattress top and determine how many inches you want your quilt to hang over each side of the bed. Adjust border widths as needed; additional yardage may be required.

STRAIGHT SETS

Throw: 50" x 64"
  Block setting: 3 x 4
  Sashing: ⅝ yard
  17 rectangles, 12½" x 12½" (A)
  Cornerstones: ⅛ yard
  6 squares, 2½" x 2½" (B)
  Border and binding: 1¾ yards
  2 strips, 4½" x 57", for sides
  2 strips, 4½" x 51", for top/bottom
  5 strips, 2¼" x 51", for binding
  Backing: 3¼ yards
  Batting: 54" x 72"

Twin: 62" x 90"
  Block setting: 4 x 6
  Sashing: 1⅛ yards
  38 rectangles, 12½" x 12½" (A)
  Cornerstones: ⅛ yard
  15 squares, 2½" x 2½" (B)
  Border and binding: 2½ yards
  2 strips, 4½" x 85", for sides
  2 strips, 4½" x 65", for top/bottom
  4 strips, 2¼" x 81", for binding
  Backing: 5⅞ yards
  Batting: 70" x 98"

Queen: 90" x 90"
  Block setting: 6 x 6
  Sashing: 1⅝ yards
  60 rectangles, 12½" x 12½" (A)
  Cornerstones: ¼ yard
  25 squares, 2½" x 2½" (B)
  Border and binding: 2¾ yards
  2 strips, 4½" x 85", for sides
  2 strips, 4½" x 93", for top/bottom
  5 strips, 2¼" x 77", for binding
  Backing: 8¾ yards
  Batting: 98" x 98"

King: 104" x 90"
  Block setting: 7 x 6
  Sashing: 1⅞ yards
  71 rectangles, 12½" x 12½" (A)
  Cornerstones: ¼ yard
  30 squares, 2½" x 2½" (B)
  Border and binding: 3⅛ yards
  2 strips, 4½" x 85", for sides
  2 strips, 4½" x 107", for top/bottom
  4 strips, 2¼" x 102", for binding
  Backing: 8¾ yards
  Batting: 112" x 98"

DIAGONAL SETS

◻ = *Cut in half diagonally.*

⊠ = *Cut into quarters diagonally.*

Throw: 59" x 76"
Block setting: 3 x 4
Setting squares and triangles: 2 yards
    6 squares, 12½" x 12½" (A)
    3 squares, 18¼" x 18¼" ⊠ (B)
      (You'll have 2 extra triangles.)
    2 squares, 9⅜" x 9⅜" ◻ (C)
Border and binding: 2¼ yards
    2 strips, 4½" x 71", for sides
    2 strips, 4½" x 62", for top/bottom
    5 strips, 2¼" x 59", for binding
Backing: 5 yards
Batting: 67" x 84"

Twin: 76" x 93"
Block setting: 4 x 5
Setting squares and triangles: 3 yards
    12 squares, 12½" x 12½" (A)
    4 squares, 18¼" x 18¼" ⊠ (B)
      (You'll have 2 extra triangles.)
    2 squares, 9⅜" x 9⅜" ◻ (C)
Border and binding: 2¾ yards
    2 strips, 4½" x 88", for sides
    2 strips, 4½" x 79", for top/bottom
    5 strips, 2¼" x 73", for binding
Backing: 7½ yards
Batting: 84" x 101"

Queen: 93" x 93"
Block setting: 5 x 5
Setting squares and triangles: 3⅜ yards
    16 squares, 12½" x 12½" (A)
    4 squares, 18¼" x 18¼" ⊠ (B)
    2 squares, 9⅜" x 9⅜" ◻ (C)
Border and binding: 3 yards
    2 strips, 4½" x 88", for sides
    2 strips, 4½" x 96", for top/bottom
    5 strips, 2¼" x 79", for binding
Backing: 9 yards
Batting: 101" x 101"

King: 110" x 93"
Block setting: 6 x 5
Setting squares and triangles: 4¼ yards
    20 squares, 12½" x 12½" (A)
    5 squares, 18¼" x 18¼" ⊠ (B)
      (You'll have 2 extra triangles.)
    2 squares, 9⅜" x 9⅜" ◻ (C)
Border and binding: 3½ yards
    2 strips, 4½" x 88", for sides
    2 strips, 4½" x 113", for top/bottom
    4 strips, 2¼" x 107", for binding
Backing: 9 yards
Batting: 118" x 101"

Playing with Blocks

Sometimes it's hard to visualize how a quilt will look when multiples of the same block are set together side by side. A lovely secondary pattern may emerge. Or, sometimes you may want to introduce a second block to mix things up.

Below and on the following pages are several examples of quilts you could make using block patterns in this book. Some of the designs feature just one block repeated for a dramatic effect. Others alternate two different blocks to create an interesting design.

These examples are just a few of the hundreds of possibilities just waiting to be stitched into your next fabulous quilt!

Texas Circle Around, page 75
Birthday Girl, page 35

Rising Star 1, page 22

Full Bloom, page 103

Faire la Bise, page 12

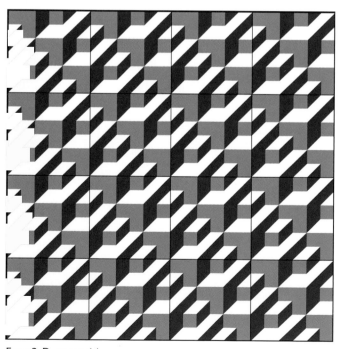

Easy 3-D, page 44

Star Flight, page 71
Tile Works, page 76

Homestead Album, page 50

Scarlet Days, page 65

Infinity, page 50

Twist and Shout, page 77

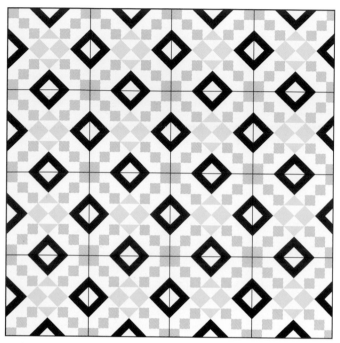

Follow Me Home, page 46

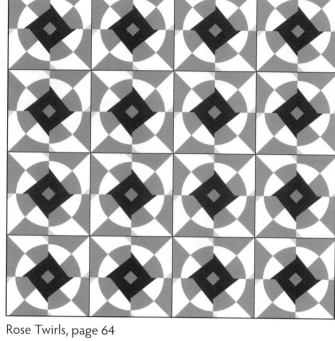

Rose Twirls, page 64

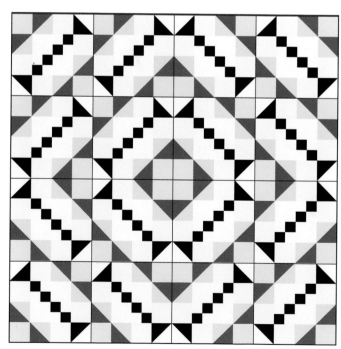

Candlestick, page 37

Companion Star, page 97
Star Checks, page 69

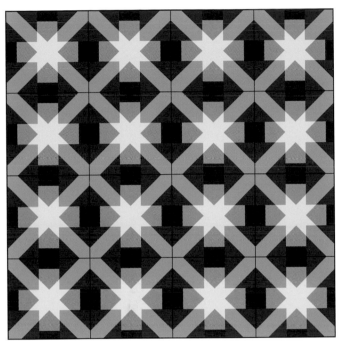

Star Across, page 69

Isobel's Flight, page 84

Isobel's Flight, page 84

Vanishing Squares, page 79

Quiltmaking Techniques

If the construction techniques used in the blocks are unfamiliar to you, here you'll find the basic information you need.

APPLIQUÉ

The instructions for each block call for the appliqué method used by the designer. To convert between fusible designs and turned-edge appliqué, you may need to reverse the patterns. No seam allowances are given on the appliqué patterns. You'll need to add them for turned-edge appliqué patterns.

Use a stabilizer on the back to support machine stitching that's dense (such as satin stitching) and to keep the fabric from tunneling. Choose a stabilizer that matches the weight of the fabric. After the appliqué is complete, gently remove the stabilizer.

FUSIBLE APPLIQUÉ

Raw-edge appliqué using paper-backed fusible web is a fast and easy way to appliqué. Because appliqué designs are drawn on the paper side of the fusible web, and then flipped when ironed onto the fabric, you may need to reverse the appliqué patterns prior to tracing the designs. (We have indicated where patterns have already been reversed.) Add ³⁄₁₆" underlap allowance to those edges that lie under another appliqué.

Trace the pattern pieces, also drawing the needed underlap allowances, on the paper side of a fusible web, leaving at least ½" between all the pieces. Cut about ³⁄₁₆" outside each drawn line.

To eliminate stiffness, try this variation for pieces larger than 1": Cut out the center of the fusible web ¼" inside the drawn line, making a ring of fusible web.

Following the manufacturer's directions, iron the web, paper side up, to the wrong side of the fabric. Cut out the shape exactly on the drawn line. Carefully pull away the paper backing. Fuse the pieces to the background as shown in the placement diagram.

To finish the raw edges, machine satin stitch with a colored thread, or zigzag or blanket-stitch using matching or invisible thread. (See "Embroidery Stitches" on page 126.)

TURNED-EDGE APPLIQUÉ

It's helpful to have as many bias edges as possible on the perimeter of your appliqué pieces; it makes the edges easier to turn under and stitch smoothly in place. Trace the pattern onto freezer paper or template plastic and cut on the seam line to make a template. Place the template face up on the right side of the fabric (face down on the right side for a reversed appliqué) and lightly draw around it. Cut out each appliqué about ³⁄₁₆" outside the marked line.

On inward curves, clip the ³⁄₁₆" allowance almost to the marked seam line. Turn under the allowances and finger-press.

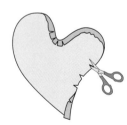

Pin or baste the appliqués on the background fabric. To appliqué by hand, use a blind stitch and a thread color that matches the appliqué.

To appliqué by machine, use a narrow zigzag or blind hem stitch and a matching or invisible thread.

If the background fabric shows through the appliqué, carefully cut away the background fabric to within ³⁄₁₆" of the appliqué or use two layers of appliqué fabric to prevent showthrough.

PERFECT APPLIQUÉ CIRCLES

Trace the circle pattern onto lightweight interfacing. Pin the interfacing to the right side of the fabric.

Stitch over the drawn line. Cut about ³⁄₁₆" outside of the drawn line. Carefully clip slits up to the stitching line, about every ¼" to ½" along the edge.

Pull the interfacing away from the fabric and carefully cut a slit in the interfacing. Pull the fabric through the interfacing to turn the circle right side out. Use a blunt instrument inside the circle to smooth out the edges. Press the circle and position in place. Finish by hand or machine stitching around the appliqué.

BIAS STRIPS

Bias strips are cut at a 45° angle to the straight grain of the fabric. They are stretchy and therefore ideal for creating curved appliqué stems.

Make your first cut by aligning a 45° guideline on your acrylic ruler with the cut edge or selvage of your fabric. Use this new bias edge to cut strips the required width.

Prepare bias strips for appliqué by folding them in half lengthwise, wrong sides together. Stitch ¼" from the raw edges. Offset the seam allowances; press toward the center. Trim the seam allowances to ⅛".

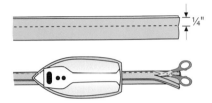

NARROW BIAS STEMS

With the wrong side facing up, place the left edge of the ⅜" bias strip along the marked placement line. Leaving about ⅛" unsewn at the ends, sew the strip in place ⅛" from the left raw edge.

Using a mixture of half water and half liquid starch, paint the right edge of the strip. Carefully fold the right edge over to the sewn line and iron it in place. A high-temperature craft iron is helpful for this step.

Fold the bias stem over one more time to cover the raw edge on the left. Tuck under ends that won't be buried under other appliqué pieces. Using matching thread and a blind stitch, appliqué the left edge of the stem.

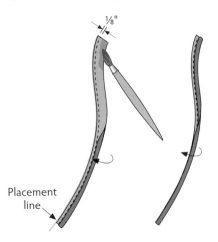

Placement line

CURVED PIECING

Cut pieces using a small-bladed rotary cutter to maneuver the curves.

With right sides together, pin the convex piece to the inside (concave) curve of the second piece at the middle, the ends, and a few places in between. Sew with the concave piece on top, stopping frequently with the needle down to adjust the fabric to lie flat under the needle and presser foot. After stitching, press the seam allowances toward the convex piece.

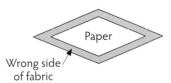

ENGLISH PAPER PIECING

With this method, every fabric piece is basted around a stiff piece of paper, and then the edges of prepared pieces are whipstitched together. Two templates are needed: one from which to cut the papers and one from which to cut the fabric pieces. Alternatively, you can purchase packages of die-cut paper foundations to save time.

Use the dashed lines of the pattern to make one plastic template (for papers); use the solid lines to make a plastic template (for fabric pieces). Using the smaller template, trace and cut one piece of stiff paper for each piece in the design. Using the larger template, trace and cut the number of fabric pieces needed.

Paper

Wrong side of fabric

Center the paper template on the wrong side of the fabric; pin together. Fold the first seam allowances over the edge of the paper template and hold in place. Baste the seam allowances through all thicknesses. When you reach the end of the seam allowance, fold over

the next seam allowance and continue stitching. Continue in this manner, making sharp folds at each corner, until all the seam allowances are basted in place. For some shapes, the folding will create tails; leave the tails hanging out as shown. Backstitch at the end to secure the stitches. Repeat for each piece needed.

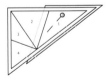

Baste.

To assemble the block, place the pieces right sides together. With a single strand of thread, whipstitch them together from corner to corner, catching only the folded edges. Repeat to join all pieces. When all edges have been joined, clip the basting threads and remove them from each piece. Carefully pull out the paper templates. You can reuse the templates.

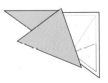

Whipstitch

FOUNDATION PIECING

Make paper copies of each foundation. Sew pieces to the foundation in numerical order. Center the fabric under #1 extending beyond the seam allowances, wrong side of the fabric to the unprinted side of the paper, and pin in place from the paper side.

Turn the fabric side up. Using a piece of fabric sufficient to cover #2 and its seam allowances, position piece #2 right sides together on piece #1 as shown, so that the fabric's edge extends at least ¼" into the #2 area. Pin in place.

Set a very short stitch length on your sewing machine (18 to 20 stitches per inch or 1.5 mm). Turn the unit paper side up. Stitch through the paper and the fabric layers along the printed seam line, beginning and ending ¼" beyond the ends of the line.

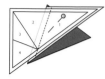

Turn the unit to the fabric side. Trim the seam allowances to approximately ¼". Press the fabric open to cover #2 and the seam allowances.

Repeat this process to complete the blocks or sections, allowing at least ¼" beyond the edge of the paper. Use a rotary cutter and ruler to trim ¼" outside the seam line of the foundation, creating a seam allowance. Once all the seams around a foundation section have been sewn, remove the paper foundations.

TRIANGLE SQUARES

With right sides together and the lighter fabric on top, pair one square of each color called for to make the triangle square. On the lighter square, draw a diagonal line from corner to corner.

Stitch ¼" from both sides of the line. Cut apart on the marked line.

With the darker fabric up, open out the top piece and press the unit. Each pair of squares will yield two units.

QUARTER-SQUARE TRIANGLES

With right sides together and the lighter fabric on top, pair one square of each color fabric called for to make the quarter-square-triangle units. On the lighter piece, draw a diagonal line from corner to corner. Stitch ¼" from both sides of the line. Cut apart on the marked line to make two triangle squares.

With the darker fabric up, open out the top piece and press the unit. Cut both triangle squares in half diagonally as shown.

Referring to the diagram, join the appropriate halves to make two units.

FAST FLYING GEESE

Align two small squares on opposite corners of a large square, right sides together. Draw a diagonal line as shown, and then stitch ¼" from both sides of the line. Cut apart on the marked line.

With the small squares on top, open out the small squares and press the unit. On the remaining corner of each of these units, align a small square. Draw a line from corner to corner and sew ¼" from both sides of the line.

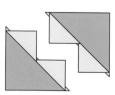

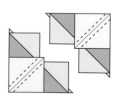

Cut on the marked lines, open the small squares, and press. Each set of one large square and four small squares makes four flying-geese units.

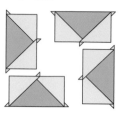

STITCH AND FLIP

Align a square on a corner of a larger square, a rectangle, or a pieced unit as called for in the block instructions. Mark a diagonal line on the square from corner to corner and sew on the marked line. Trim the seam allowances to ¼" as shown. Flip the square open and press.

SET-IN SEAMS (Y SEAMS)

A set-in piece is inserted in an angle formed by the union of two other pieces.

On the wrong side of the pieces, use a ruler to mark an accurate ¼" seam line in all corners. With right sides together, align the edges of two pieces and pin through the ¼" marks of both pieces. Sew the seam between the ¼" marks, backstitching to secure the seam at the beginning and end.

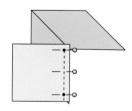

Pivot the set-in piece so the adjacent edge aligns with the edge of the third piece. Matching seams, pin in place. Starting exactly where the previous seam ended, sew two stitches, and then back-stitch, taking care not to stitch into the seam allowance. Stitch to the outer edge.

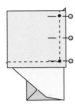

YO-YOS

Using the circle diameter called for in the pattern (approximately twice the finished yo-yo size plus ½"), make a template. Circle patterns are given on the enclosed disk. On the wrong side of the fabric, use the template to trace a circle. Cut out the circle on the marked line.

Turn under a scant ¼" to the wrong side of the fabric. Sew a short basting stitch around the circle, leaving a knot and thread tail at the beginning of the circle.

Pull on the threads to gather the fabric, making sure the right side of the fabric is on the outside of the yo-yo. Take a few stitches to secure the gathering stitches and tie off. Clip the threads close to the knot. Flatten the yo-yo with gathered edge in center.

BEADING

Use a beading thread to secure beads to your work. Make a knot after every bead or after every few beads to ensure their security.

Single bead

Because bugle beads edges can be sharp and sometimes cut the thread, it helps to buffer them with a round bead at each end.

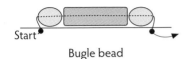

Bugle bead

EMBROIDERY STITCHES

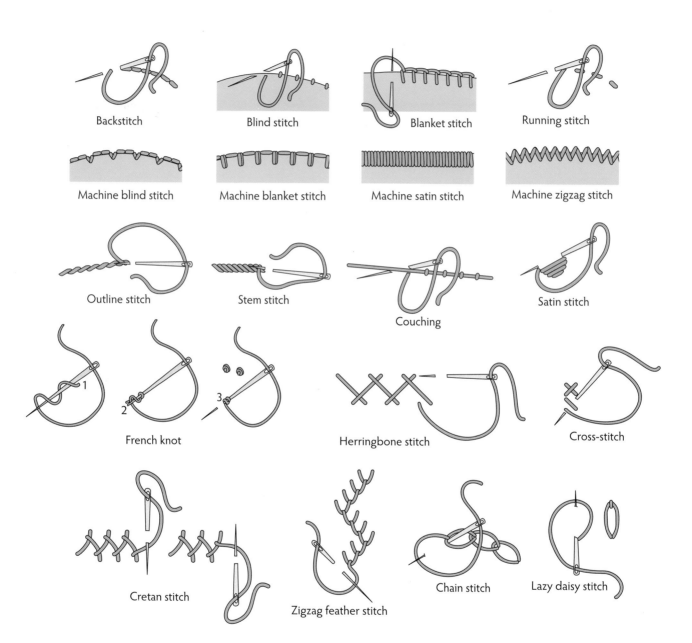

Backstitch

Blind stitch

Blanket stitch

Running stitch

Machine blind stitch

Machine blanket stitch

Machine satin stitch

Machine zigzag stitch

Outline stitch

Stem stitch

Couching

Satin stitch

French knot

Herringbone stitch

Cross-stitch

Cretan stitch

Zigzag feather stitch

Chain stitch

Lazy daisy stitch

Block Index by Designer